"These essays are brilliant. No feminist, male or female, can afford to miss them."
—Carolyn Kizer

"Nancy Mairs has insisted upon telling the truth and the world may well, as predicted, split open. Although hers has been a life of illness, both physical and emotional, she offers here testimony to the connection between 'illness' and women's confined destiny and internalized guilt. These essays are not only honest, searingly so, they are witty, immensely readable, and they pay no homage to that imprisoner of female lives, the appropriate."
—Carolyn Heilbrun

"To read *Plaintext* is like doing some high, hard mountain-climbing with a fearless and experienced guide. Nancy Mairs's unacceptant, insistent re-examination and revaluation of self, language, and ideas—a central strategy of feminist thought—brings the reader exhilarated through a series of risks worth taking."
—Ursula K. Le Guin

"There are triumphs here—of will, style, candor, thought and even form."
—Art Seidenbaum, *Los Angeles Times*

"Reading *Plaintext* is much like reading a fascinating private journal—one well worth making public. Courageous candidness."
—*Kirkus Reviews*

"Here is transcendence. . . . *Plaintext* is a road map to Mairs's reconciliation and recovery, one we can follow along the way to our own healing."
—Faye Moskowitz, *Belles Lettres*

"Nancy Mairs has the poet's easy access to the unconscious, and the poet's gift for the meaningfully concrete. . . . in her ability to plumb the travail of the simultaneously talented and womanly woman of our time, to feel and tell the contradictions of intelligent female lives, Mairs is a brilliantly 'crippled' writer indeed."
—Beryl Lieff Benderly, *Washington Post*

Plaintext

ESSAYS BY
NANCY MAIRS

PERENNIAL LIBRARY

Harper & Row, Publishers, New York
Cambridge, Philadelphia, San Francisco, Washington
London, Mexico City, São Paulo, Singapore, Sydney

A hardcover edition of this book is published by the University of Arizona Press. It is here reprinted by arrangement with the University of Arizona Press.

The following essays, in somewhat modified form, originally appeared in the cited journals: "On Being a Cripple" in *MSS*; "On Touching by Accident" in *A Room of One's Own*; "On Being a Scientific Booby" in *Arizona English Bulletin*; "Woman With Full Red Lips" (as "A Moslem Seeks Her Future") in *Sojourner*; and "A Letter to Matthew" in *Frontiers*.

First PERENNIAL LIBRARY edition published 1987.

Library of Congress Cataloging-in-Publication Data

Mairs, Nancy, 1943–
    Plaintext.

    I. Title.
[PS3563.A386P5   1987]   814'.54   86-46085
ISBN 0-06-097094-4 (pbk.)

87 88 89 90 91 MPC 10 9 8 7 6 5 4 3 2 1

for both my Annes
the mother and the daughter
who have made a woman of me

and for Ken Marsh
who has kept me alive long enough
to experience the condition

Contents

Anyone who comes to us with a symptom, believes in it. If he asks for our assistance or help, it is because he believes that the symptom is capable of saying something, and that it only needs deciphering. The same goes for a woman, except that it can happen that one believes her effectively to be saying something. That's when things get stopped up—to believe *in*, one believes *her*. It's what's called love.

Jacques Lacan, *Feminine Sexuality*

Preface

A few years ago I almost died by my own hand, and when I woke from that disagreeable event, I recognized for the first time that I was fully and solely responsible for my existence. Not, you may say if you have made it already, a remarkable discovery. But I had got to the age of thirty-seven—with a husband and children and mortgage payments and college degrees and students of my own and any number of other cultural emblems of maturity—having managed not to make it. These essays enact that responsibility, however belatedly discovered, in the terms in which I can understand it: as a writer of my life.

I owe more debts of gratitude for help in this difficult project than I can ever hope to acknowledge adequately. At The University of Arizona, the first is to Edward Abbey, in whose workshop I began, almost by accident, to write essays. I am grateful, too, to Mary Carter, Robert Houston, and Steve Orlen of the creative writing program, who saw merit in my work before I did, and to Barbara Babcock, Jerrold Hogle, and Patrick O'Donnell, who formed my dissertation committee and encouraged me to write this book. My greatest debt is to Susan Hardy Aiken, my dissertation director, under whose tutelage I finally emerged as a feminist, and under whose demands I have stretched much further beyond my self-imposed limitations than I could ever have dreamed or dared on my own.

Beyond the academy I have found support as well. My aunt, the poet Jean Pedrick, and her husband, Frank Kefferstan, have several times given me a room of my own at Skimmilk Farm in New Hampshire, not to mention more zucchini than any human being could reasonably hope for. My special thanks to them, and to the poets in the Monday Workshop there, who laughed in all the right places.

I was fortunate to be able to join the community at the Bread Loaf Writers' Conference as a Time, Inc., Scholar in Nonfiction in 1982 and the William P. Sloane Fellow in Nonfiction in 1984. There, I received generous encouragement from many writers, especially David Bain, John Gardner, Robert Pack, Linda Pastan, Ron Powers, and Hilma Wolitzer. Their excitement over the essays infected me and produced the stamina I needed in order to stay with the work even at its most painful.

The labors of making a book have been infinitely eased by my patient and able typist, Majill Weber.

To my husband and children goes my deepest gratitude, for giving me the life that is this text.

NANCY MAIRS

SELF

On Having Adventures

The other day I had lunch with a friend, another writer, in the back room of one of those California-type restaurants as common now as golden arches all over the country. Our relationship has been played out almost entirely in such a setting—whether The Egg Garden, as now, or Delectables or The Blue Willow or La Bocca—the two of us at a small table in a small, cool, dim room, surrounded by syngoniums and pothos, talking shop over iced tea and spinach-mushroom quiche—or brie and strawberries or asparagus crêpes or gazpacho. As an agoraphobe who, fifteen years ago, could not have crossed the sill of my apartment, and who even now suffers wayward attacks of breathlessness in movie theatres and lecture halls and even friends' homes, I find that conducting a relationship in a California-type restaurant contains a certain risk and creates a certain headiness associated more often, perhaps, with rappelling down a cliff face or buying a winning ticket in the New Hampshire lottery than with eating bread and cheese in public. When I've pulled the whole thing off, as I usually do nowadays, when I've actually paid the check and walked back to my car, I feel the pleasant lethargy that follows the excitement of a hard job well done.

This day we were talking, of course, about writing, of which neither of us had been doing very much, and my friend was bemoaning the flatness of his life. He needed to have adventures in order to write, he said, and he wasn't having any.

"Ah," I said sententiously. I find it easy to be sententious with this friend because, although he is only six years younger than I, he thinks and acts another six years younger, thereby throwing me smack into my matronizing mode. "Ah, but it all depends on how you construe adventures."

"I suppose." He stabbed at a cherry tomato.

"I mean," I told him, "I've come into these bettas—you know, Siamese fighting fish—and I can even have adventures with those." I was serious. I have a low adventure threshold, rather like having a low pain threshold. In fact, I have a low pain threshold as well, as this friend has good reason to know, and perhaps the two are related. I am wounded easily, but I am just as easily delighted.

Thus encouraged, my friend allowed that he might well have had an adventure in Albuquerque the week before. He went on to tell me about going to a bar where a friend of his is a waitress and meeting the band there, who took him out to breakfast at four a.m. and dedicated songs to him the next night . . . a narrative so fraught with potential noisy adventures that I felt dizzy and pained in my head just contemplating them, though clearly he still wasn't sure he had had an adventure at all. The trouble with having a low adventure threshold is that everything that crosses it may be an adventure, and thus you may be inundated and swept away by the events of a life that seems to others as still as a stagnant pond. Think about a drop of water from that pond under a microscope, however: the adventurous life.

Cats are the most adept creatures I know at living the adventurous life. Which is odd, in a way, since they spend the bulk of their hours curled up asleep on bedspreads or on one's favorite clothes (black for white cats, white for black cats). But awake, they are open to every adventure, no matter how shadowy: They stare, stalk, lurk, pounce, tug, tussle, bound. Since many of their adventures involve eating something, often something you'd rather not think about, they also crunch. And wash.

Of all the cats who have lived with us, Burton Rustle was the most exquisite artist of adventure. He came to us squalling, rescued out of a tree, a bobtail spotted-tabby kitten, absolutely adorable, living proof that nature makes her babies cute so that adults won't kill or abandon them. He grew astonishingly fat and spent even more time than most cats sleeping, not curled up, but rather stretched out on his back with his legs akimbo. But when he came to, the adventures began, one after another, like chapters in a cliff-hanger. Burton Rustle and the Blue Afghan. Burton Rustle and the Fig-Eaters. Burton Rustle and the Water Swirling in the Toilet. Burton Rustle and the Orange Dust Mop. Burton Rustle and the Folding Table Under the Bed. Burton Rustle and the Blind Snake Lost in the Shag Rug. We don't know what his last adventure was, but it must have involved a car, for we found him under Anne's bed one morning with his head crushed—one eye loose and swollen with blood, jaws twisted, teeth broken, tongue thick and protruding—still alive and crying at us in a cracked voice. We rushed him to the veterinarian, who gave him a quick injection, and then took him home in a box and buried him under a tree in our yard. Sometimes I stop by the brick marker, on which I painted "Burton Rustle, beloved cat of Anne Mairs, 1979–1981," and salute him, this jaunty, corpulent figure who knew how to make every waking moment crackle with tension, with suspense, who knew the value of the grand gesture and injected high drama into low life.

Burton's is the way I choose to live my life, open to every possibility and promise, no matter how ordinary it seems to those who are living other lives. Take the bettas, for instance. In fact, a few weeks ago I'd cheerfully have given you the bettas. I've had all kinds of pets—cats and hamsters and snakes and dogs, mice, guinea pigs, horny toads, even tarantulas and black widows—but never tropical fish. I think tropical fish are dumb. But Anne's friend Emily bred her bettas and gave Anne one of the—what's the right term?—litter? covey? pride? clutch? Anyway, Alpha Betta turned out to be a female, an outcome as disappointing in the case of tropical fish as it seems to be in so many other instances, so Emily gave Anne Omega as well. Now the two live side by side, in one-gallon pickle jars bought at our favorite pizza place, among the plants on the mantel. Fortunately bettas, like carp, are accustomed to stagnant waters, having originated in Siamese rice paddies, so they need no fancy filters and lights, just an occasional change of water and a sprinkling of fish flakes each night. They spend their lives circling sinuously. Off and on Omega, staring through the glass of his pickle jar and of her pickle jar, will catch a glimpse of Alpha, and then his fins flare and erect into gorgeous iridescent royal-blue sails and he twists and darts in a mad display. Usually Alpha is not looking.

Very fine, you say. You have little finny friends, your very own lower life forms. But what about adventures? Actually, I just told you an adventure, but maybe it was a little low-key. Maybe you have to stand transfixed for many minutes at a time, day after day, in front of two pickle jars in order for an adventure to take shape. Let me try one with a bit more action.

Friends going to Germany for the summer left to our care a couple of dozen plants and a guppy, a tiny phosphorescent orange and lime crea-

5

ture, whom we named Spot and dumped into Alpha's jar. We did not notice right away, the guppy being so very tiny, that Alpha, in her dashes at him, was tearing Spot's fins, and by the time we did, and removed him to his own apothecary jar, Spot was shaped pretty much like an eel, wriggling madly but not getting very far. The Rescue of Spot, with the attendant anxious observation to see whether he would survive his denuding, was decidedly an adventure. I am pleased to report that although his dorsal and ventral fins are still rather ragged, Spot's tail fin seems to have regenerated completely, and he darts ceaselessly around his apothecary jar in an aimless, frenetic, guppylike dither.

Nearly ten years ago, I was told that I had a brain tumor, and this experience, I think, changed my relationship to adventure forever. I thought that I was going to die, that all my adventures were over. I did not, it turned out, have a brain tumor, but rather multiple sclerosis, which meant that, although they were not over, the nature of my adventures would have to change. Each morning that I wake up, that I get out of bed, is a fresh event, something that I might not have had. Each gesture that I make carries a weight of uncertainty, demands significant attention: buttoning my shirt, changing a light bulb, walking down stairs. I might not be able to do it this time. Inevitably the minutiae of my life have had to assume dramatic proportions. If I could not love them, delight in them, they would likely drown me in rage and in self-pity, that tempting, obliterating sea.

I admire the grand adventures of others. I read about them with zest. With Peter Matthiessen I have trekked across the Himalaya to the Crystal Mountain and seen no snow leopard. One blistering July I moved with John McPhee to Eagle, Alaska, above the Arctic Circle. I have trudged with Annie Dillard up, down, into, and across Tinker Creek in all seasons. David Bain has hiked me along a hundred and ten miles of Philippine coast, and Edward Abbey has paddled me down the Colorado River. I've ridden on the back of Robert Pirsig's motorcycle, climbed ninety-five feet to George Dyson's tree house, grown coffee in Kenya with Isak Dinesen. With wonder I contemplate the actions of these rugged and courageous figures, who can strike out on trips of miles—two, two hundred and fifty, three thousand—ready to endure cold, fatigue, human and natural hostility, ready not just to endure but to celebrate.

But as for me, I can no longer walk very far from the armchair in which I read. I'll never make it to Tibet. Maybe not even to Albuquerque. Some days I don't even make it to the back yard. And yet I'm unwilling to forgo the adventurous life: the difficulty of it, even the pain, the suspense and fear, and the sudden brief lift of spirit that graces—unexpectedly, inexplicably—the pilgrimage. If I am to have it too, then I must change the terms by which it is lived. And so I do. I refine adventure, make it smaller and smaller, until it fits into this little toad that struggles through the jungle of clover under my bare feet. And now, whether I am feeding fish flakes to my bettas or crawling across the dining room helping Burton look for his blind snake, lying wide-eyed in the dark battling yet another bout of depression, cooking a chicken, gathering flowers from the garden at the Farm, meeting a friend for lunch at The Blue Willow, I am always having the adventures that are mine to have.

On Being a Cripple

To escape is nothing. Not to escape is nothing.
Louise Bogan

The other day I was thinking of writing an essay on being a cripple. I was thinking hard in one of the stalls of the women's room in my office building, as I was shoving my shirt into my jeans and tugging up my zipper. Preoccupied, I flushed, picked up my book bag, took my cane down from the hook, and unlatched the door. So many movements unbalanced me, and as I pulled the door open I fell over backward, landing fully clothed on the toilet seat with my legs splayed in front of me: the old beetle-on-its-back routine. Saturday afternoon, the building deserted, I was free to laugh aloud as I wriggled back to my feet, my voice bouncing off the yellowish tiles from all directions. Had anyone been there with me, I'd have been still and faint and hot with chagrin. I decided that it was high time to write the essay.

First, the matter of semantics. I am a cripple. I choose this word to name me. I choose from among several possibilities, the most common of which are "handicapped" and "disabled." I made the choice a number of years ago, without thinking, unaware of my motives for doing so. Even now, I'm not sure what those motives are, but I recognize that they are complex and not entirely flattering. People—crippled or not—wince at the word "cripple," as they do not at "handicapped" or "disabled." Perhaps I want them to wince. I want them to see me as a tough customer, one to whom the fates/gods/viruses have not been kind, but who can face the brutal truth of her existence squarely. As a cripple, I swagger.

But, to be fair to myself, a certain amount of honesty underlies my choice. "Cripple" seems to me a clean word, straightforward and precise. It has an honorable history, having made its first appearance in the Lindisfarne Gospel in the tenth century. As a lover of words, I like the accuracy with which it describes my condition: I have lost the full use of my limbs. "Disabled," by contrast, suggests any incapacity, physical or mental. And I certainly don't like "handicapped," which implies that I have deliberately been put at a disadvantage, by whom I can't imagine (my God is not a Handicapper General), in order to equalize chances in the great race of life. These words seem to me to be moving away from my condition, to be widening the gap between word and reality. Most remote is the recently coined euphemism "differently abled," which partakes of the same semantic hopefulness that transformed countries from "undeveloped" to "underdeveloped," then to "less developed," and finally to "developing" nations. People have continued to starve in those countries during the shift. Some realities do not obey the dictates of language.

Mine is one of them. Whatever you call me, I remain crippled. But I don't care what you call me, so long as it isn't "differently abled," which strikes me as pure verbal garbage designed, by its ability to describe anyone, to describe no one. I subscribe to George Orwell's thesis that "the slovenliness of our language makes it easier for us to have foolish thoughts." And I refuse to participate in the degeneration of the language to the extent that I deny that I have lost anything in the course of this calamitous disease; I refuse to pretend that the only differences between you and me are the various ordinary ones that distinguish any one person from another. But call me "disabled" or "handicapped" if you like. I have long since grown accustomed to them; and if they are vague, at least they hint at the truth. Moreover, I use them myself. Society is no readier to accept crippledness than to accept death, war, sex, sweat, or wrinkles. I would never refer to another person as a cripple. It is the word I use to name only myself.

I haven't always been crippled, a fact for which I am soundly grateful. To be whole of limb is, I know from experience, infinitely more pleasant and useful than to be crippled; and if that knowledge leaves me open to bitterness at my loss, the physical soundness I once enjoyed (though I did not enjoy it half enough) is well worth the occasional stab of regret. Though never any good at sports, I was a normally active child and young adult. I climbed trees, played hopscotch, jumped rope, skated, swam, rode my bicycle, sailed. I despised team sports, spending some of the wretchedest afternoons of my life, sweaty and humiliated, behind a field-hockey stick and under a basketball hoop. I tramped alone for miles along the bridle paths that webbed the woods behind the house I grew up in. I swayed through countless dim hours in the arms of one man or another under the scattered shot of light from mirrored balls, and gyrated through countless more as Tab Hunter and Johnny Mathis gave way to the Rolling Stones, Creedence Clearwater Revival, Cream. I walked down the aisle. I pushed baby carriages, changed tires in the rain, marched for peace.

When I was twenty-eight I started to trip and drop things. What at first seemed my natural clumsiness soon became too pronounced to shrug off. I consulted a neurologist, who told me that I had a brain tumor. A battery of tests, increasingly disagreeable, revealed no tumor. About a year and a half later I developed a blurred spot in one eye. I had, at last, the episodes "disseminated in space and time" requisite for a diagnosis: multiple sclerosis. I have never been sorry for the doctor's initial misdiagnosis, however. For almost a week, until the negative results of the tests were in, I thought that I was going to die right away. Every day for the past nearly ten years, then, has been a kind of gift. I accept all gifts.

Multiple sclerosis is a chronic degenerative disease of the central nervous system, in which the myelin that sheathes the nerves is somehow eaten away and scar tissue forms in its place, interrupting the nerves' signals. During its course, which is unpredictable and uncontrollable, one may lose vision, hearing, speech, the ability to walk, control of bladder and/or bowels, strength in any or all extremities, sensitivity to touch, vibration, and/or pain, potency, coordination of movements—the list of possibilities is lengthy and, yes, horrifying. One may also lose one's sense of humor. That's the easiest to lose and the hardest to survive without.

In the past ten years, I have sustained some of these losses. Characteristic of MS are sudden attacks, called exacerbations, followed by remissions, and these I have not had. Instead, my disease has been slowly progressive. My left leg is now so weak that I walk with the aid of a brace and a cane; and for distances I use an Amigo, a variation on the electric wheelchair that looks rather like an electrified kiddie car. I no longer have much use of my left hand. Now my right side is weakening as well. I still have the blurred spot in my right eye. Overall, though, I've been lucky so far. My world has, of necessity, been circumscribed by my losses, but the terrain left me has been ample enough for me to continue many of the activities that absorb me: writing, teaching, raising children and cats and plants and snakes, reading, speaking publicly, about MS and depression, even playing bridge with people patient and honorable enough to let me scatter cards every which way without sneaking a peek.

Lest I begin to sound like Pollyanna, however, let me say that I don't like having MS. I hate it. My life holds realities—harsh ones, some of them—that no right-minded human being ought to accept without grumbling. One of them is fatigue. I know of no one with MS who does not complain of bone-weariness; in a disease that presents an astonishing variety of symptoms, fatigue seems to be a common factor. I wake up in the morning feeling the way most people do at the end of a bad day, and I take it from there. As a result, I spend a lot of time *in extremis* and, impatient with limitation, I tend to ignore my fatigue until my body breaks down in some way and forces rest. Then I miss picnics, dinner parties, poetry readings, the brief visits of old friends from out of town. The offspring of a puritanical tradition of exceptional venerability, I cannot view these lapses without shame. My life often seems a series of small failures to do as I ought.

I lead, on the whole, an ordinary life, probably rather like the one I would have led had I not had MS. I am lucky that my predilections were already solitary, sedentary, and bookish—unlike the world-famous French cellist I have read about, or the young woman I talked with one long afternoon who wanted only to be a jockey. I had just begun graduate school when I found out something was wrong with me, and I have remained, interminably, a graduate student. Perhaps I would not have if I'd thought I had the stamina to return to a full-time job as a technical editor; but I've enjoyed my studies.

In addition to studying, I teach writing courses. I also teach medical students how to give neurological examinations. I pick up freelance editing jobs here and there. I have raised a foster son and sent him into the world, where he has made me two grandbabies, and I am still escorting my daughter and son through adolescence. I go to Mass every Saturday. I am a superb, if messy, cook. I am also an enthusiastic laundress, capable of sorting a hamper full of clothes into five subtly differentiated piles, but a terrible housekeeper. I can do italic writing and, in an emergency, bathe an oil-soaked cat. I play a fiendish game of Scrabble. When I have the time and the money, I like to sit on my front steps with my husband, drinking Amaretto and smoking a cigar, as we imagine our counterparts in Leningrad and make sure that the sun gets down once more behind the sharp childish scrawl of the Tucson Mountains.

This lively plenty has its bleak complement, of course, in all the things I can no longer do. I will never run again, except in dreams, and one day I may have to write that I will never walk again. I like to go camping, but I can't follow George and the children along the trails that wander out of a campsite through the desert or into the mountains. In fact, even on the level I've learned never to check the weather or try to hold a coherent conversation: I need all my attention for my wayward feet. Of late, I have begun to catch myself wondering how people can propel themselves without canes. With only one usable hand, I have to select my clothing with care not so much for style as for ease of ingress and egress, and even so, dressing can be laborious. I can no longer do fine stitchery, pick up babies, play the piano, braid my hair. I am immobilized by acute attacks of depression, which may or may not be physiologically related to MS but are certainly its logical concomitant.

These two elements, the plenty and the privation, are never pure, nor are the delight and wretchedness that accompany them. Almost every pickle that I get into as a result of my weakness and clumsiness—and I get into plenty—is funny as well as maddening and sometimes painful. I recall one May afternoon when a friend and I were going out for a drink after finishing up at school. As we were climbing into opposite sides of my car, chatting, I tripped and fell, flat and hard, onto the asphalt parking lot, my abrupt departure interrupting him in mid-sentence. "Where'd you go?" he called as he came around the back of the car to find me hauling myself up by the door frame. "Are you all right?" Yes, I told him, I was fine, just a bit rattly, and we drove off to find a shady patio and some beer. When I got home an hour or so later, my daughter greeted me with "What have you done to yourself?" I looked down. One elbow of my white turtleneck with the green froggies, one knee of my white trousers, one white kneesock were blood-soaked. We peeled off the clothes and inspected the damage, which was nasty enough but not alarming. That part wasn't funny: The abrasions took a long time to heal, and one got a little infected. Even so, when I think of my friend talking earnestly, suddenly, to the hot thin air while I dropped from his view as though through a trap door, I find the image as silly as something from a Marx Brothers movie.

13

I may find it easier than other cripples to amuse myself because I live propped by the acceptance and the assistance and, sometimes, the amusement of those around me. Grocery clerks tear my checks out of my checkbook for me, and sales clerks find chairs to put into dressing rooms when I want to try on clothes. The people I work with make sure I teach at times when I am least likely to be fatigued, in places I can get to, with the materials I need. My students, with one anonymous exception (in an end-of-the-semester evaluation), have been unperturbed by my disability. Some even like it. One was immensely cheered by the information that I paint my own fingernails; she decided, she told me, that if I could go to such trouble over fine details, she could keep on writing essays. I suppose I became some sort of bright-fingered muse. She wrote good essays, too.

The most important struts in the framework of my existence, of course, are my husband and children. Dismayingly few marriages survive the MS test, and why should they? Most twenty-two- and nineteen-year-olds, like George and me, can vow in clear conscience, after a childhood of chicken pox and summer colds, to keep one another in sickness and in health so long as they both shall live. Not many are equipped for catastrophe: the dismay, the depression, the extra work, the boredom that a degenerative disease can insinuate into a relationship. And our society, with its emphasis on fun and its association of fun with physical performance, offers little encouragement for a whole spouse to stay with a crippled partner. Children experience similar stresses when faced with a crippled parent, and they are more helpless, since parents and children can't usually get divorced. They hate, of course, to be different from their peers, and the child whose mother is tacking down the aisle of a school auditorium packed with proud parents like a Cape Cod dinghy in a stiff breeze jolly well stands out in a crowd. Deprived of legal divorce, the child can at least deny the mother's disability, even her existence, forgetting to tell her about recitals and PTA meetings, refusing to accompany her to stores or church or the movies, never inviting friends to the house. Many do.

But I've been limping along for ten years now, and so far George and the children are still at my left elbow, holding tight. Anne and Matthew vacuum floors and dust furniture and haul trash and rake up dog droppings and button my cuffs and bake lasagna and Toll House cookies with just enough grumbling so I know that they don't have brain fever. And far from hiding me, they're forever dragging me by racks of fancy

14

clothes or through teeming school corridors, or welcoming gaggles of friends while I'm wandering through the house in Anne's filmy pink babydoll pajamas. George generally calls before he brings someone home, but he does just as many dumb thankless chores as the children. And they all yell at me, laugh at some of my jokes, write me funny letters when we're apart—in short, treat me as an ordinary human being for whom they have some use. I think they like me. Unless they're faking. . . .

Faking. There's the rub. Tugging at the fringes of my consciousness always is the terror that people are kind to me only because I'm a cripple. My mother almost shattered me once, with that instinct mothers have—blind, I think, in this case, but unerring nonetheless—for striking blows along the fault-lines of their children's hearts, by telling me, in an attack on my selfishness, "We all have to make allowances for you, of course, because of the way you are." From the distance of a couple of years, I have to admit that I haven't any idea just what she meant, and I'm not sure that she knew either. She was awfully angry. But at the time, as the words thudded home, I felt my worst fear, suddenly realized. I could bear being called selfish: I am. But I couldn't bear the corroboration that those around me were doing in fact what I'd always suspected them of doing, professing fondness while silently putting up with me because of the way I am. A cripple. I've been a little cracked ever since.

Along with this fear that people are secretly accepting shoddy goods comes a relentless pressure to please—to prove myself worth the burdens I impose, I guess, or to build a substantial account of goodwill against which I may write drafts in times of need. Part of the pressure arises from social expectations. In our society, anyone who deviates from the norm had better find some way to compensate. Like fat people, who are expected to be jolly, cripples must bear their lot meekly and cheerfully. A grumpy cripple isn't playing by the rules. And much of the pressure is self-generated. Early on I vowed that, if I had to have MS, by God I was going to do it well. This is a class act, ladies and gentlemen. No tears, no recriminations, no faint-heartedness.

One way and another, then, I wind up feeling like Tiny Tim, peering over the edge of the table at the Christmas goose, waving my crutch, piping down God's blessing on us all. Only sometimes I don't want to play Tiny Tim. I'd rather be Caliban, a most scurvy monster. Fortunately, at home no one much cares whether I'm a good cripple or a bad cripple as long as I make vichyssoise with fair regularity. One evening several years ago, Anne was reading at the dining-room table while I cooked dinner. As I opened a can of tomatoes, the can slipped in my left hand and juice spattered me and the counter with bloody spots. Fatigued and infuriated, I bellowed, "I'm so sick of being crippled!" Anne glanced at me over the top of her book. "There now," she said, "do you feel better?" "Yes," I said, "yes, I do." She went back to her reading. I felt better. That's about all the attention my scurviness ever gets.

Because I hate being crippled, I sometimes hate myself for being a cripple. Over the years I have come to expect—even accept—attacks of violent self-loathing. Luckily, in general our society no longer connects deformity and disease directly with evil (though a charismatic once told me that I have MS because a devil is in me) and so I'm allowed to move largely at will, even among small children. But I'm not sure that this revision of attitude has been particularly helpful. Physical imperfection, even freed of moral disapprobation, still defies and violates the ideal, especially for women, whose confinement in their bodies as objects of desire is far from over. Each age, of course, has its ideal, and I doubt that ours is any better or worse than any other. Today's ideal woman, who lives on the glossy pages of dozens of magazines, seems to be between the ages of eighteen and twenty-five; her hair has body, her teeth flash white, her breath smells minty, her underarms are dry; she has a career but is still a fabulous cook, especially of meals that take less than twenty minutes to prepare; she does not ordinarily appear to have a husband or children; she is trim and deeply tanned; she jogs, swims, plays tennis, rides a bicycle, sails, but does not bowl; she travels widely, even to out-of-the-way places like Finland and Samoa, always in the company of the ideal man, who possesses a nearly identical set of characteristics. There are a few exceptions. Though usually white and often blonde, she may be black, Hispanic, Asian, or Native American, so long as she is unusually sleek. She may be old, provided she is selling a laxative or is Lauren Bacall. If she is selling a detergent, she may be married and have a flock of strikingly messy children. But she is never a cripple.

Like many women I know, I have always had an uneasy relationship with my body. I was not a popular child, largely, I think now, because I was peculiar: intelligent, intense, moody, shy, given to unexpected actions and inexplicable notions and emotions. But as I entered adolescence, I believed myself unpopular because I was homely: my breasts too flat, my mouth too wide, my hips too narrow, my clothing never quite right in fit or style. I was not, in fact, particularly ugly, old photographs inform me, though I was well off the ideal; but I carried this sense of self-alienation with me into adulthood, where it regenerated in response to the depredations of MS. Even with my brace I walk with a limp so pronounced that, seeing myself on the videotape of a television program on the disabled, I couldn't believe that anything but an inchworm could make progress humping along like that. My shoulders droop and my pelvis thrusts forward as I try to balance myself upright, throwing my frame into a bony S. As a result of contractures, one shoulder is higher than the other and I carry one arm bent in front of me, the fingers curled into a claw. My left arm and leg have wasted into pipe-stems, and I try always to keep them covered. When I think about how my body must look to others, especially to men, to whom I have been trained to display myself, I feel ludicrous, even loathsome.

At my age, however, I don't spend much time thinking about my appearance. The burning egocentricity of adolescence, which assures one that all the world is looking all the time, has passed, thank God, and I'm generally too caught up in what I'm doing to step back, as I used to, and watch myself as though upon a stage. I'm also too old to believe in the accuracy of self-image. I know that I'm not a hideous crone, that in fact, when I'm rested, well dressed, and well made up, I look fine. The self-loathing I feel is neither physically nor intellectually substantial. What I hate is not me but a disease.

I am not a disease.

And a disease is not—at least not singlehandedly—going to determine who I am, though at first it seemed to be going to. Adjusting to a chronic incurable illness, I have moved through a process similar to that outlined by Elizabeth Kübler-Ross in *On Death and Dying*. The major difference—and it is far more significant than most people recognize—is that I can't be sure of the outcome, as the terminally ill cancer patient can. Research studies indicate that, with proper medical care, I may achieve a "normal" life span. And in our society, with its vision of death as the ultimate evil, worse even than decrepitude, the response to such news is, "Oh well, at least you're not going to *die*." Are there worse things than dying? I think that there may be.

I think of two women I know, both with MS, both enough older than I to have served me as models. One took to her bed several years ago and has been there ever since. Although she can sit in a high-backed wheel-chair, because she is incontinent she refuses to go out at all, even though incontinence pants, which are readily available at any pharmacy, could protect her from embarrassment. Instead, she stays at home and insists that her husband, a small quiet man, a retired civil servant, stay there with her except for a quick weekly foray to the supermarket. The other woman, whose illness was diagnosed when she was eighteen, a nursing student engaged to a young doctor, finished her training, married her doctor, accompanied him to Germany when he was in the service, bore three sons and a daughter, now grown and gone. When she can, she travels with her husband; she plays bridge, embroiders, swims regularly; she works, like me, as a symptomatic-patient instructor of medical students in neurology. Guess which woman I hope to be.

At the beginning, I thought about having MS almost incessantly. And because of the unpredictable course of the disease, my thoughts were always terrified. Each night I'd get into bed wondering whether I'd get out again the next morning, whether I'd be able to see, to speak, to hold a pen between my fingers. Knowing that the day might come when I'd be physically incapable of killing myself, I thought perhaps I ought to do so right away, while I still had the strength. Gradually I came to understand that the Nancy who might one day lie inert under a bed-sheet, arms and legs paralyzed, unable to feed or bathe herself, unable to reach out for a gun, a bottle of pills, was not the Nancy I was at present, and that I could not presume to make decisions for that future Nancy, who might well not want in the least to die. Now the only provision I've made for the future Nancy is that when the time comes—and it is likely to come in the form of pneumonia, friend to the weak and the old—I am not to be treated with machines and medications. If she is unable to communicate by then, I hope she will be satisfied with these terms.

Thinking all the time about having MS grew tiresome and intrusive, especially in the large and tragic mode in which I was accustomed to considering my plight. Months and even years went by without catastrophe (at least without one related to MS), and really I was awfully busy, what with George and children and snakes and students and poems, and I hadn't the time, let alone the inclination, to devote myself to being a disease. Too, the richer my life became, the funnier it seemed, as though there were some connection between largesse and laughter, and so my tragic stance began to waver until, even with the aid of a brace and a cane, I couldn't hold it for very long at a time.

After several years I was satisfied with my adjustment. I had suffered my grief and fury and terror, I thought, but now I was at ease with my lot. Then one summer day I set out with George and the children across the desert for a vacation in California. Part way to Yuma I became aware that my right leg felt funny. "I think I've had an exacerbation," I told George. "What shall we do?" he asked. "I think we'd better get the hell to California," I said, "because I don't know whether I'll ever make it again." So we went on to San Diego and then to Orange, up the Pacific Coast Highway to Santa Cruz, across to Yosemite, down to Sequoia and Joshua Tree, and so back over the desert to home. It was a fine two-week trip, filled with friends and fair weather, and I wouldn't have missed it for the world, though I did in fact make it back to California two years later. Nor would there have been any point in missing it, since in MS, once the symptoms have appeared, the neurological damage has been done, and there's no way to predict or prevent that damage.

The incident spoiled my self-satisfaction, however. It renewed my grief and fury and terror, and I learned that one never finishes adjusting to MS. I don't know now why I thought one would. One does not, after all, finish adjusting to life, and MS is simply a fact of my life—not my favorite fact, of course—but as ordinary as my nose and my tropical fish and my yellow Mazda station wagon. It may at any time get worse, but no amount of worry or anticipation can prepare me for a new loss. My life is a lesson in losses. I learn one at a time.

And I had best be patient in the learning, since I'll have to do it like it or not. As any rock fan knows, you can't always get what you want. Particularly when you have MS. You can't, for example, get cured. In recent years researchers and the organizations that fund research have started to pay MS some attention even though it isn't fatal; perhaps they have begun to see that life is something other than a quantitative phenomenon, that one may be very much alive for a very long time in a life that isn't worth living. The researchers have made some progress toward understanding the mechanism of the disease: It may well be an autoimmune reaction triggered by a slow-acting virus. But they are nowhere near its prevention, control, or cure. And most of us want to be cured. Some, unable to accept incurability, grasp at one treatment after another, no matter how bizarre: megavitamin therapy, gluten-free diet, injections of cobra venom, hypothermal suits, lymphocytopharesis, hyperbaric chambers. Many treatments are probably harmless enough, but none are curative.

The absence of a cure often makes MS patients bitter toward their doctors. Doctors are, after all, the priests of modern society, the new shamans, whose business is to heal, and many an MS patient roves from one to another, searching for the "good" doctor who will make him well. Doctors too think of themselves as healers, and for this reason many have trouble dealing with MS patients, whose disease in its intransigence defeats their aims and mocks their skills. Too few doctors, it is true, treat their patients as whole human beings, but the reverse is also true. I have always tried to be gentle with my doctors, who often have more at stake in terms of ego than I do. I may be frustrated, maddened, depressed by the incurability of my disease, but I am not diminished by it, and they are. When I push myself up from my seat in the waiting room and stumble toward them, I incarnate the limitation of their powers. The least I can do is refuse to press on their tenderest spots.

This gentleness is part of the reason that I'm not sorry to be a cripple. I didn't have it before. Perhaps I'd have developed it anyway—how could I know such a thing?—and I wish I had more of it, but I'm glad of what I have. It has opened and enriched my life enormously, this sense that my frailty and need must be mirrored in others, that in searching for and shaping a stable core in a life wrenched by change and loss, change and loss, I must recognize the same process, under individual conditions, in the lives around me. I do not deprecate such knowledge, however I've come by it.

All the same, if a cure were found, would I take it? In a minute. I may be a cripple, but I'm only occasionally a loony and never a saint. Anyway, in my brand of theology God doesn't give bonus points for a limp. I'd take a cure; I just don't need one. A friend who also has MS startled me once by asking, "Do you ever say to yourself, 'Why me, Lord?' " "No, Michael, I don't," I told him, "because whenever I try, the only response I can think of is 'Why not?' " If I could make a cosmic deal, who would I put in my place? What in my life would I give up in exchange for sound limbs and a thrilling rush of energy? No one. Nothing. I might as well do the job myself. Now that I'm getting the hang of it.

On Touching by Accident

Those of us who would be suicides come at odd bits of knowledge about the failings of the human heart. Not necessarily literal heart failure, of course: A good many of us stop short of that point, for one reason or another. Virginia Woolf, for instance, who swallowed a lethal dose of veronal in 1913, did not take her final walk, into the River Ouse with her pockets full of stones, until 1941. We may survive. We often do. The failings I'm talking about have to do not with death, which is another matter altogether ("the one experience," Woolf noted, "I shall never describe"), but with life—with lives. The last time I tried to kill myself, a number of things happened to me, most of them predictable and some of them not very pleasant. But one of them was odd enough that still, months later, I return to the thought of it, amused and puzzled and more than a little anxious about its significance.

I am a depressive. Researchers know surprisingly little about my condition, which is called "unipolar" depression to distinguish it from "bipolar" or manic depression. It may be caused by a chemical imbalance in the brain. It occurs cyclically, and each person has his own cycle—or, more likely, her own cycle, since far more women suffer from depression than men. No one knows why, though some very good reasons have been proposed. (A thorough review of depression in women is Maggie Scarf's *Unfinished Business: Pressure Points in the Lives of Women* [New York: Ballantine Books, 1980].) Depression is characterized by disturbances in normal physiological functions like eating and sleeping and by suicidal thoughts or acts arising from a sense of personal worthlessness and despair. As a rule, a depressive does not attempt suicide until she begins to feel better, probably because, in the depths of depression, she has felt too powerless even to kill herself. Several doctors have told me, with a good deal of satisfaction, that I am a textbook case. I do not like being a textbook case. I feel dull. Nonetheless, every so often I fall off the edge of the world into a void even blacker than the one that kept medieval sailors in charted waters; and as soon as I begin to emerge, I grab for the bottle of pills.

Just so the last time. Gradually my consciousness filled with the image of a thin sharp blade drawing again and again across the blue veins in my wrist. This image is symbolic only—except for one youthful attempt, I have never tried to slash my wrists and would not now choose to do so—and I am never entirely free from it. But when it becomes so repetitive that it screens out the faces and voices of people around me, even my own face in the mirror, then I know I am in mortal danger. (Wonderful how such clichés take on their original purity and force in a literal context.) I kept checking myself for signs of survival: I polished my fingernails and had a permanent; I bought a director's chair in which to sit in the sun and a soft plum-colored velveteen blazer; I sent a short story to *The New Yorker*. People who do such things, I reasoned, do not commit suicide. Finally, however, exhausted by the moment-to-moment decisions to stay alive, I decided on a Tuesday that I would kill myself on Friday night.

From then on, I was frantically busy. I had to sort through the tottering piles on my desks at home and in my office. I had to catch up on the teaching duties I had neglected and plan activities for the rest of the semester, so that whoever took over could do so with the least possible disruption of my students' learning. I had to write a long letter to George, listing the names and numbers of people to notify, reminding him that my body was to be donated for research into multiple sclerosis, detailing the distribution of my personal effects. During that time I also did a couple of interviews for a television program about the disabled that I was hosting. I had a drink with a friend. I invited my daughter to spend a night with me in the apartment to which I'd moved a few weeks before and bought her a pink striped shirt and a pair of purple jeans at the same time I bought my blazer.

By Friday night I was tired. I thought about staying home from the Hallowe'en party I'd said I'd go to, but finally I put on my new blazer and went (and all evening harlequins and witches and men with gigantic bosoms and miniskirts asked me, "Where's your costume?" and I said, carefully, each time, "You're looking at it"). I had a pretty good time. To be sure, the man with whom I was in love, who had recently thrown me over (another pure and forceful cliché), was there, annihilating me; but then, a well-known novelist flirted with me, so I must have had some substance. I was kissed by a pirate and possibly also by a devil. I didn't drink much. I left early.

When I got home, the back yard of my little apartment building, where I parked my car, was dark; but there was a moon, and I'd left my porch light on, so I could find my door. As I stuck the key into the lock, a figure danced out of the darkness—a clown, I think, in a pink ruffled suit—and pleaded, "Oh, can I use your bathroom? I'm at this party over there"—vague gesture—"and the line to the bathroom is *miles* long and I've been drinking all this *beer* and I'm about to *burst* and . . . " "Sure," I said, swinging the door in. "It's in there." While she peed torrentially, I turned on the radio, opened a beer, and put down fresh food for Bête Noire, who was twisting around my ankles like a dervish. The clown flushed and came out, yanking at her ruffles. "This is so *hard* to get in and out of," she moaned. "Oh, thank you. You saved my *life*. I just couldn't have waited any longer." She was pink and plump. I didn't think she was old enough for the beer. "Oh, *there* you are," she called to a shadow that loomed on the doorstep, and off she bounded, recounting my heroic rescue of her in her moment of greatest need.

I closed the door behind her. I went into the bathroom and started taking Elavil while I washed my face and undressed. I went back into the tidy white bedroom/living room/kitchen/study and sat down at my desk. Still taking the Elavil, three by three, I finished my letter to George and tried to write in my journal, but my vision was too badly blurred. I dropped the bottle of Elavil and couldn't see to pick up the small yellow tablets. That clumsiness probably saved my life. That, and Bête Noire. I had at first thought I would turn on my stove and heater, which had no pilot lights, and thus hasten the work of the drug. But Bête was so tiny that I knew that the gas would kill her long before me, and I couldn't bear the thought of her black body still and lifeless. By this time I had no sense of myself or anyone else as a living creature; and when, later, a psychiatrist asked if I hadn't tried to call for help after taking all those pills, I had to say that I didn't know there was anyone to call; yet I couldn't kill the kitten.

George found me eighteen hours later and took me to the emergency room, where, after a few hours on a heart monitor and the obligatory psychiatric interview, I was pronounced a survivor and sent home. I had at some point roused having to go to the bathroom and, unable to get even to my hands and knees, had dragged myself around my apartment, battering my body and smearing the floor with blood and urine; but I heal quickly. Before long the bruises faded and the scabs fell off. I was still shaky but no longer suicidal. I had let a lot of my responsibilities slide, so I threw myself into activity and forgot the whole mess as much and as quickly as possible.

Then one day, six weeks or so later, when I was having lunch with a friend and we were swapping stories of failed love and suicide, I saw suddenly the round pink ruffled form of the little clown dancing through my door and into my bathroom. I had wholly forgotten her and the young man waiting for her in the shadows under my cedar trees. I was startled by the memory—so quick, so complete—startled and amused, and I began to describe it to my friend. Just then, though, the man who had thrown me over, with whom I was still in love, asked if he might join us, and naturally we had to speak of other things. I never finished my story about the clown.

I have thought of her often since then, however. She entered my life so lightly, this child, needing only a place to empty her bladder so that she wouldn't disgrace herself, at just the moment when I was planning to leave, though she couldn't have known that. And I wonder whether I have done just the same thing myself, wandering through some other's desolation in my costume—tight jeans, soft shirt, dusky velveteen blazer, cane—needing some quick favor on my way. How many times? And when?

On Being a Scientific Booby

My daughter is dissecting a chicken. Her first. Her father, whose job this usually is, has been derelict in his duties, and my hands are now too weak to dissect much more than a zucchini. If she wants dinner (and she does), she will make this pale, flabby carcass into eight pieces I can fit into the skillet. I act as coach. To encourage her, I tell her that her great-great-grandfather was a butcher. This is true, not something I have made up to con her into doing a nasty job.

Now that she's gotten going, she is having a wonderful time. She has made the chicken crow and flap and dance all over the cutting board, and now it lies quiet under her short, strong fingers as she slices the length of its breastbone. She pries back the ribs and peers into the cavity. "Oh, look at its mesenteries!" she cries. I tell her I thought mesentery was something you got from drinking the water in Mexico. She pokes at some filmy white webs. Mesenteries, she informs me, are the membranes that hold the chicken's organs in place. My organs too. She flips the chicken over and begins to cut along its spine. As her fingers search out joints and the knife severs wing from breast, leg from thigh, she gives me a lesson in the comparative anatomy of this chicken and the frog she and her friend Emily have recently dissected at school.

I am charmed by her enthusiasm and self-assurance. Since she was quite small, she has talked of becoming a veterinarian, and now that she is approaching adulthood, her purpose is growing firmer. During this, her junior year in a special high school, she is taking a college-level introductory course in biology. I took much the same course when I was a freshman in college. But if I entered that course with Anne's self-confidence, and I may very well have done so, I certainly had none of it by the time I wrote the last word of my final examination in my blue book and turned it in the following spring. As the result of Miss

White and the quadrat report, I am daunted to the point of dysfunction by the notion of thinking or writing "scientifically."

That woman—damn that woman!—turned me into a scientific cripple, and did so in the name of science at a prestigious women's college that promised to school me in the liberal arts that I might "have life and have it abundantly." And really, I have had it abundantly, so I suppose I oughtn't to complain if it's been a little short in *Paramecia* and *Amanita phalloides* and *Drosophila melanogaster,* whose eyes I have never seen.

Still, Miss White should not have been allowed to teach freshman biology because she had a fatal idiosyncracy (fatal, that is, to the courage of students, not to herself, though I believe she is dead now of some unrelated cause): She could not bear a well-written report. One could be either a writer or a scientist but not both, she told me one November afternoon, the grey light from a tall window sinking into the grain of the dark woodwork in her cramped office in the old Science Building, her fingers flicking the sheets of my latest lab write-up. She was washing her hands of me, I could tell by the weariness of her tone. She didn't even try to make me a scientist. For that matter, she didn't even point to a spot where I'd gone wrong and show me what she wanted instead. She simply wrinkled her nose at the odor of my writing, handed me the sheets, and sent me away. We never had another conference. At the end of the semester, I wrote my quadrat report, and Miss White failed it. She allowed me to rewrite it. I wrote it again, and she failed it again. Neither of us went for a third try.

All the same, I liked my quadrat, which was a twenty-by-twenty plot in the College Woods behind the Library. Mine was drab compared to some others: Pam Weprin's, I remember, had a brook running through it, in which she discovered goldfish. It turned out that her magical discovery had a drab explanation: In a heavy rain the water from Peacock Pond backed up and spilled its resident carp into the brook. Even so, her quadrat briefly held an excitement mine never did. Mine was, in fact, as familiar as a living room, since I had spent large portions of my youth tramping another such woods sixty miles north. The lichen grew on the north side of the trees. In the rain the humus turned black and rank. Afterwards, a fallen log across one corner would sprout ears of tough, pale fungus.

Each freshman biology student received a quadrat. There were enough of us that we had to double up, but I never met my quadrat-mate or even knew her name. It occurs to me now that I ought to have found out, ought to have asked her what she got on her quadrat report, but I was new to failure and knew no ways to profit from it. I simply did as I was told—visited my quadrat to observe its progress through the seasons and wrote up my observations—and then discovered that I had somehow seen and spoken wrong. I wish now that I had kept the report. I wonder exactly what I said in it. Probably something about ears of fungus. Good God.

With a D+ for the first semester I continued, perversely, to like biology, but I also feared it more and more. Not the discipline itself. I pinned and opened a long earthworm, marveling at the delicately tinted organs. I dissected a beef heart, carefully, so as not to spoil it for stuffing and roasting at the biology department's annual beef-heart feast. For weeks I explored the interior of my rat, which I had opened neatly, like the shutters over a window. He was a homely thing, stiff, his fur yellow and matted from formaldehyde, and because he was male, not very interesting. Several students got pregnant females, and I envied them the intricate organs, the chains of bluish-pink fetuses. At the end of each lab, I would reluctantly close the shutters, swaddle my rat in his plastic bag, and slip him back into the crock.

No, biology itself held more fascination and delight than fear. But with each report I grew more terrified of my own insidious poetic nature, which Miss White sniffed out in the simplest statement about planaria or left ventricles. Years later, when I became a technical editor and made my living translating the garbled outbursts of scientists, I learned that I had done nothing much wrong. My understanding was limited, to be sure, but Miss White would have forgiven me ignorance, even stupidity I think, if I had sufficiently muddled the language. As it was, I finished biology with a C−, and lucky I was to get it, since the next year the college raised the passing grade from C− to C. I have always thought, indeed, that the biology department awarded me a passing grade simply so that they wouldn't have to deal with me another year.

And they didn't. Nor did anyone else. I never took another science course, although I surprised myself long afterward by becoming, perforce and precipitously, a competent amateur herpetologist. My husband arrived home one afternoon with a shoebox containing a young bull snake, or gopher snake as this desert variety is called, which he had bought for a quarter from some of his students at a school for

27

emotionally disturbed boys so that they wouldn't try to find out how long a snake keeps wriggling without its head. This was Ferdinand, who was followed by two more bull snakes, Squeeze and Beowulf, and by a checkered garter snake named Winslow J. Tweed, a black racer named Jesse Owens, a Yuma king snake named Hrothgar, and numerous nameless and short-lived blind snakes, tiny and translucent, brought to us by our cats Freya, Burton Rustle, and Vanessa Bell. I grew so knowledgeable that when my baby boa constrictor, Crictor, contracted a respiratory ailment, I found that I was more capable of caring for him than were any of the veterinarians in the city. In fact, I learned, veterinarians do not do snakes; I could find only one to give Crictor the shot of a broad-spectrum antibiotic he needed.

So I do do snakes. I have read scientific treatises on them. I know that the Latin name for the timber rattlesnake is *Crotalus horridus horridus*. I know that Australia has more varieties of venomous snakes than any other continent, among them the lethal sea snakes and the willfully aggressive tiger snake. I know how long one is likely to live after being bitten by a mamba (not long). I read the treatises; but I don't, of course, write them. Although as a technical editor I grew proficient at unraveling snarls in the writing of scientists, I have never, since Miss White, attempted scientific experimentation or utterance.

Aside from my venture into herpetology, I remain a scientific booby. I mind my stupidity. I feel diminished by it. And I know now that it is unnecessary, the consequence of whatever quirk of fate brought me into Miss White's laboratory instead of Miss Chidsey's or Dr. McCoy's. Miss White, who once represented the whole of scientific endeavor to me, was merely a woman with a hobbyhorse. I see through her. Twenty years later, I am now cynical enough to write a quadrat report badly enough to pass her scrutiny, whereas when I had just turned seventeen I didn't even know that cynicism was an option—knowledge that comes, I suppose, from having life abundantly. I've learned, too, that Miss White's bias, though unusually strong, was not peculiar to herself but arose from a cultural rift between the humanities and the sciences resulting in the assumption that scientists will naturally write badly, that they are, in fact, rhetorical boobies. Today I teach technical writing. My students come to me terrified of the word-world from which they feel debarred, and I teach them to breach the boundaries in a few places, to step with bravado at least a little way inside. Linguistic courage is the gift I can give them.

In return, they give me gifts that I delight in—explanations of vortex centrifuges, evaluations of copper-smelting processes, plans for extracting gums from paloverde beans. These help me compensate for my deficiencies, as do the works of the popularizers of science. Carl Sagan. Loren Eiseley. Lewis Thomas and his reverential reflections subtitled *Notes of a Biology Watcher.* Stephen Jay Gould. James Burke and Jacob Bronowski. Pierre Teilhard de Chardin. John McPhee, who has made me love rocks. Isaac Asimov. Elaine Morgan. I watch television too. *Nova. Odyssey. The Undersea World of Jacques Cousteau. The Body in Question.* But always I am aware that I am having translated for me the concepts of worlds I will never now explore for myself. I stand with my toes on the boundaries, peering, listening.

Anne has done a valiant job with the chicken. She's had a little trouble keeping its pajamas on, and one of the thighs has a peculiar trapezoidal shape, but she's reduced it to a workable condition. I brown it in butter and olive oil. I press in several cloves of garlic and then splash in some white wine. As I work, I think of the worlds Anne is going to explore. Some of them are listed in the college catalogues she's begun to collect: "Genetics, Energetics, and Evolution"; "Histology of Animals"; "Vertebrate Endocrinology"; "Electron Microscopy"; "Organic Synthesis"; "Animal Morphogenesis."

Anne can write. No one has yet told her that she can be a scientist or a writer but not both, and I trust that no one ever will. The complicated world can ill afford such lies to its children. As she plunges from my view into the thickets of calculus, embryology, and chemical thermodynamics, I will wait here for her to send me back messages. I love messages.

LIFE

Woman With Full Red Lips

Lamia and I are sitting in my office, as we have done dozens of times during the past several months, only this time our roles are reversed: She is instructing me. I am ordinarily Lamia's tutor, hired because I combine familiarity with Middle English language and literature with the practice of Roman Catholicism, and she has been required, as part of her graduate program, to take a course in Middle English. The language has presented few problems, especially since excellent translations exist of most of the works she is studying; but the literature, rooted in the European tradition, is nearly meaningless to a young Moslem woman. I am essentially a cultural interpreter, who can explain the irony of Gawain's lavish feast of fish on a fast day, the reason that Launcelot can never attain the vision of the Holy Grail, the interpenetration of the cult of the Virgin and the ideal of courtly love. In the course of our conversations, however, she has shared with me so much of her background, experiences, and values that I feel sure of having learned at least as much as she has. Now I've asked her to bring together for me some of the bits and pieces I've gleaned in the course of our talks, particularly with regard to her womanhood.

I am at a disadvantage, and there seems to be nothing I can do about it. We are speaking in my language, which Lamia has studied for ten years and in which she converses fluently, even idiomatically. I don't know her language at all—I don't think I'd recognize it as Arabic if I overheard it, in the way that I would recognize Spanish, French, German—and I haven't read any Arabic literature even in translation. We are sitting on the campus of a large university in a sprawling Southwestern city, surrounded by emblems of my culture: Outside my office students are lounging on the mall, men and women together, in almost equal states of undress on this hot April afternoon, playing Frisbee, eating popcorn and Fritos and ice cream cones, calling out plans for Friday-night beer blasts at nearby dormitories and fraternities. Lamia walks among them every day. I have never left this country, this culture, much less gone so far as the Middle East. She understands far more about me than I can hope to understand about her, and I keep feeling that I am asking the wrong questions. I don't know what to do with her answers. I jot them down like strokes of color on an impressionist painting, knowing I can't make an accurate representation but hoping I will see eventually not merely face and form but something of what animates the face and form.

Lamia is twenty-five years old, a graduate of a small women's university in the Middle East, working toward the Ph.D. in English literature here. All Arabic names have meanings, she tells me; hers means "woman with full red lips." I think that she is beautiful, but she tells me she is not because her countrymen, like Americans, prefer slender women, and she is heavy. Who, then, would they think beautiful, I ask.

"You," she replies instantly.

"Why?" I can't help but laugh, startled.

"Because you're thin and white."

From my new and uneasy perch as a beautiful woman, not just a scrawny one who doesn't get enough sun, I admire her face, broad and handsome, with clear brown skin and dark eyes. She wears a good deal of makeup, carefully applied; and her clothes are expensive and tasteful. Today she is wearing a dress and jacket of a soft semi-sheer white fabric embroidered in white, and the contrast with her skin and nearly black hair and eyes is subtly startling. She talks with animation and laughs readily and richly.

I ask her to begin by telling me a little about her background, and she starts with her home, a city of over a million inhabitants, growing at the rate of about a thousand new residents a month and changing so rapidly that when she goes back to visit, she doesn't bother to adjust to the differences, since by the time she returns permanently, all will have changed again. There she was born, the second of four children, two boys and two girls. Both her brothers are mentally retarded, so she is in the unusual position of being her father's "hope" even though she is not male. Her sister, Nadia, a year younger than she, has joined her here to work on a doctorate in economics.

34

She grew up in an extended family, as many as eighty people living together in a complex of three graceful four-story stone-and-wood houses in a section of the city which, with rapid growth and Westernization, is becoming a slum. Her grandfather and his wife, her aunts, her uncles, all took care of and disciplined her. She shows me a picture of herself with Nadia when the two were very small, two wide-eyed, serious little girls dressed in lavishly ruffled white dresses that her young aunts, as yet unmarried, made and dressed them in like live dolls. As for the discipline, it was "very strict—but very loving." The usual form of punishment was whipping; but although she remembers some children being whipped almost daily, "I wasn't a naughty child," she says, recalling only three whippings, all administered by her father, twice for lying and the third for an "emotional problem—teenage love and stuff like that—and he couldn't take it."

"He," her father, she "did not know" until she was fifteen or so. Now in his fifties, he is "a trader, a merchant," who deals mainly in leather goods and runs his own store. Although highly educated, as a young man he hated the idea of being bossed and would not work for the government. All his friends now hold high-ranking government positions; and when I ask her whether he regrets his decision to go into business, Lamia replies, "Sometimes I feel it, yes." Economically, he is "middle middle-class" (in a country with an annual per capita income of over seventeen thousand dollars); social status depends not on income, however, but on family name. "Yours is a good one?" I ask. "Yes, very good." Because he worked at night, Lamia saw her father only at "the time of punishment": "I always hated him," she says. Later, however, "he was surprised to know me"; and now he says, "The only person whom I can talk to is my daughter [Lamia]. . . . We have a lot in common."

Now, obviously, she has far more in common with her father than with her mother; for although there were always schools for boys in her country, schools for women began with Lamia's generation, so her mother is virtually uneducated. Women of her mother's generation had "tutors." They were taught to read the Koran, and a few were taught to write; the emphasis, however, was on "home economics." Lamia, by contrast, was sent when she was about three to a private girls' school, the goal of which was to provide religious education, although it offered a full curriculum. An attempt to open a similar school when her mother was young had met with overwhelming resistance. People weren't ready for such a concept, Lamia says, for "the idea that you [girls] have a life separate from their own," for the act of girls "leaving the house alone."

By Lamia's youth, though, opposition to the education of women had lessened; and not long after she started school, the government began to open schools for girls. The normal course of instruction is six years at the elementary level, followed by three years at the preparatory and three at the secondary levels. Until she was about to graduate from secondary school, Lamia didn't know that a university for women existed. It was tiny—maybe fifty students—and taught by Egyptian women, since no women from her own country were yet qualified to teach at the university level. Lamia graduated with a degree in English literature in 1977 and taught English for a year before winning a scholarship to the United States. Since no graduate program in English literature—or even in Arabic literature—existed, she had to come here in order to continue her studies.

She didn't win this point with her father without a struggle, however. Because of Western "immorality," he refused to let her come alone. Even now, her family is afraid "all the time" of her being corrupted by Westerners. I probe for the heart of their fear and finally ask if it is sexual. "Oh, yes. Sexuality is a taboo. We don't even talk about it before marriage. It does not exist at all." But surely, I say, she must at least have been told about menstruation. "I was horrified. They hadn't told me. I got my period very, very early. I was nine years old. I was terrified. They have this thing about virginity and stuff like that, and you're always told that a virgin gets blood when she first has sex, and I thought that I'd lost my virginity." I think of my daughter's first period. I was hanging clothes in the back yard when she burst through the door, waving a pair of panties.

"What does a period look like?" she asked. "Does it look like this?"

"It does indeed."

"Then I've got it." She danced back into the house to raid the sample box from Kimberly-Clark cached in her closet a year and more before.

"Do you want to tell Daddy, or shall I?" I asked when I came in from the laundry.

"You," she said. So I did, and George went in to give her a big congratulatory hug. For the rest of the day she floated through the house sighing with satisfaction, "I'm a woman. I'm a woman."

Lamia learned about other aspects of sexuality through reading and whispering with other girls; to this day, she would not discuss such matters with her mother. She does think that attitudes toward women's sexuality have changed, that sex is no longer considered merely for servicing a man and getting pregnant. Nevertheless, the leniency of Western sexual attitudes and practices is clearly seen by Lamia's family as a threat to her virtue.

Despite these fears, however, when one of her young uncles also won a scholarship, her father acquiesced to her studying in the United States, although he insisted that her mother come as well. The entourage, which settled in Los Angeles, consisted finally of Lamia, her uncle, her mother, her younger brother, a young female cousin, and an unmarried aunt. Lamia quickly finished a course in English and spent the remainder of the school year watching television "from signing on to signing off," until she was fluent in American English. Meanwhile, her uncle, burdened with the responsibility of their menage and eager to be on his own, made life so miserable that Lamia grew desperate. She couldn't bear to stay with him; neither could she remain alone and responsible for the others, none of whom spoke any English, in Los Angeles. She had friends in Tucson whose family name her father knew, so he gave her permission to move her household here.

I am astonished at her courage, and also at her curious mixture of independence and deference. She has in the past vigorously defended—not merely to me but to the public, in an article published on the editorial page of the local newspaper—the traditional Islamic view of women as scripturally lesser than men. Obviously, "lesser" doesn't mean helpless. She has required the permission of a man halfway around the world in order to move. But, permission granted, she has come five hundred miles, found a town house, enrolled her brother in a special high school, enrolled herself in the University, and assumed the role of head of a household of five.

What changes in her lifestyle, I wonder, has she experienced since leaving her country. "I don't see any change really," she says. "I come to school, I go home and just sit there." If anything, her freedom is more restricted because here she is responsible for her family. Her mother and aunt depend on her even for entertainment; since they speak no English, they cannot even watch television without translation, at which Lamia and Nadia take turns. "They cook," she comments, "but that's about all. How many times can you clean the house?" They are too frightened to leave the house without her; nor do they want her to leave except to go to school.

"Do you and Nadia ever go out by yourselves?" I ask.

"We sneak out—we never stop sneaking out. We tried once to make

37

it formal; we got into trouble, just a lot of trouble. They never believe that you're alone." If the two young women want to go out without their family, in other words, they must be secretly meeting men.

Men. I want to understand about men, and I have been puzzling about them during this conversation as I have during earlier ones, but I can't get Lamia's perceptions and attitudes to come clear. I have, I think, a pretty ordinary middle-class American background. I was educated in co-educational private and public schools and at a private women's college. I started dancing with boys when I was nine or ten at Miss James's Dancing School; I started kissing them when I was twelve or thirteen at parties; and I first fell in love with one not long before my fourteenth birthday. When I was nineteen I married the man of my choice, and perhaps the oddest feature of my experience is that I am still married to him eighteen years later. I was not a virgin on my wedding night, though I had been until a few months before. I have shared offices and classrooms with men; I have worked with them and for them. I have had affairs with a few of them, most of which have been pleasant, and friendships with many more. I suppose I like men about as well as I like anybody.

Lamia's experience of men seems very different. When I ask her about the equality of men and women, she says that of course she will receive equal pay for her work, which she will do only among women, but that equality itself is "not an issue at all. Men stay apart. A man can't just come into the room when a woman is entertaining her friends." In fact, "men stay apart" to the extent that, outside her family, Lamia has known almost none of them. Nonetheless, she delights in the thought of romance, and we laugh at the vulnerability to romantic desires we share as the result of our immersion in literature. She has, in fact, been in love with a man—seriously, secretly, and in the end painfully. The seriousness I understand, of course, and the pain as well; but I have trouble with the secrecy. It seems fundamental to any relationship between a Middle Eastern man and woman outside the bounds of marriage and family. My mother had boyfriends openly; my grandmothers had boyfriends openly; I suppose that my great-grandmothers did too, though I never asked them; now my daughter has them. The tradition of open courtship is so old in our culture, the importance of "getting a man" by one's own devices so strong, that the notion of hiding him once one has him seems, at the least, self-defeating. I was praised and petted for getting men—not beaten.

Lamia fell in love when she was seventeen with the friend of a neighbor. The old houses in her city stand one against the other with only a narrow passage between: "I would sneak out and go to that hallway and meet him." These clandestine meetings went on for five years, until the man proposed to her father and was rejected on social and economic grounds, because his parents were immigrants and he was not educated. Even then, Lamia might have escaped discovery except that the man insisted on his proposal three times; "that's when my father became suspicious," she says, that she might not be disinterested in the proposal herself. She received her third whipping. The man, "frustrated," went away and married another woman. I ask her whether she has been in love again, and she laughs. "You know how artists are—they're in love with love, I guess. So I'm always in search of such an emotion, but I've never been in such a relationship where I was swept off my feet again." Does she, I wonder, regret having had the relationship. "No, not at all. . . . I think I would have regretted marrying him, if I was to be deprived of all I'm getting right now." What would her life have been like, I want to know. "If I'd married him, after two years I'd be having my first child, then another and another." Four children, she says, are the socially accepted limit unless "you keep on getting girls"; in that case, a woman might have "seven, eight, just get a boy."

Marriage, then, is an arrangement between men, which the woman has the right to refuse but not to promote. Love is not a consideration, but in fact, Lamia tells me, "most marriages nowadays are based on love, but it's always a secret—nobody knows about it until the guy proposes. And if you're lucky enough, the family will approve." Lamia was not lucky enough. And now? She says she is too old for marriage, "down the hill" and, more important, over-educated. Very few men would "venture" to propose, and "to get such a person you have to have other qualities too—you have to be young and beautiful and maybe rich too." When I ask her whether she'd be inclined to find someone for herself, she replies, "Why not?" but "I'm not thinking of marriage at all," only of romance. As for getting married, "I prefer not to. I'm not up to the responsibility of marriage. And I hate the idea of it—I see an end in it." For others, even her sister, who "has one more year of eligibility," is "skinny," and has, Lamia feels, "a tendency to become a wife," marriage is "just the beginning. Everybody's just waiting to be taken away. That's what they want—that's the Kingdom, they call it."

When I ask whether her attitude sets her apart, she allows that she has never heard "one other woman" say what she has just said.

"What kind of future," I ask, "do you see for yourself?"

Her tone is rich and resonant: "Oh, mine own." She will probably spend five more years in the United States—"the longer, the better"—but she won't stay permanently because here she always feels like a visitor. And when she returns to her own country? "I want to work . . . to teach . . . to write . . . I see signs of a novelist in me." She keeps two journals, a formal one in Arabic and a casual one in English, and plans to write novels in Arabic and translate them herself. The arts are little known and little valued in her own country; she would like to write a critical column on the arts, perhaps for the first women's magazine, a weekly that has recently been started. She will live with her family, in the old houses if they can be saved from urban renewal. She will have friendships, openly with women, perhaps clandestinely with men. "That's why this has been such a terrific experience for me here," she says, "because all the previous contacts I had with guys—you could never tell the difference between friendship and love or just fooling around. It's very hard for you to draw a line. I never could." Here she has begun to see how one could be friends with a man.

I have expressed all these hopes. I have lived out some of them. Her realities may baffle me, but her hopes I can understand. In the middle of my cluttered, shabby office, she seems vibrant and tough and self-confident, equal to the complexities and ambivalences and, no doubt, the loneliness she will experience if she lives out her anomalous dreams, and even after she leaves, I feel her there:

"What kind of a future do you see for yourself?"

"Oh, mine own."

Ron Her Son

"Bye, Grandma," says Chris, who is not quite two, raising his round, wide-eyed face and pouting to meet my lips. "Bye, Grandma," echoes Alex, who suddenly, after a week of spurning all advances, raises his face too for a kiss. Angel is crying as I give her a hug. Ron is characteristically stiff and taciturn in the face of feeling, but he lets me put my arms around him and kiss him, and he even hugs me back a little. Then, in a swirl of arms and legs, a bobbing of heads, they are in their huge, battered station wagon, which must somehow convey them—blankets and bottles, clothes and thermos jugs and trinkets from Mexico and disposable diapers—from here to Texas and then on to Key West. The early morning is greyish and humid, unusual for Tucson in September. I stand on the porch in my nightgown and wave even after they've pulled out of sight.

What has just happened should be that commonplace of American family life, the visit of a son and his wife and their two children to Grandma and Grandpa's house. But it's not. What has just happened is, in many small ways, a miracle.

Ron is not, in fact, my son. Although biologically I am old enough to be his mother, his birth would have put a severe crimp in my high-school style—more, would have been a miracle indeed, since I remained a virgin for several years after Ron was born. Not for seven years after his birth would I actually take on motherhood, and even then people thought me (with some reason) too young. And yet he's more my son than anyone else's. George and I have owned ourselves his parents for longer than anyone else has been willing to do. He may be ours by default, but he is ours. He told me so himself, years ago, in a ragged typewritten note I find now in a file of odd documents that account piecemeal for his life with us:

To Nancy

To the one who took me in. Who give me food the one who cared for
me the one who helped me in my hour of need. Who loved me. Here
is to a wonder person. On her day, Mother's day.
HAPPY MOTHER'S DAY

Love,
Ron her son

Last comer, eldest child: orphan, waif, bad boy: survivor: son.

George found Ron at the Chazen Institute, a school for emotionally
disturbed children where he taught during our first year in Tucson. It
was, I imagine, fairly typical of such a place: the children badly housed
and fed while the director scooped out as much profit as he could and
then split for Chicago. I saw a flow chart of the organization once, in
the shape of a pyramid, with the director at the top and the students
squeezed in at the bottom, falling off the page. George did not think it a
good place for children, and so as often as he could he brought the
teenage boys he worked with home. Weekends our house was filled with
thieves and muggers, I suppose; one boy, I recall, had put his stepmother through a plate-glass window. He was large for his age. In our
house the boys were good-humored, often deferential, and very hungry.

George and I suffer from an adoption complex. Usually we have been
able to assuage our urge to shelter homeless creatures by a visit to the
local Humane Society, whence we have rescued such members of our
household as Freya and Gwydion and Vanessa Bell and Lionel Tigress
and Clifford-the-Small-Black-Dog. But occasionally we have found
ourselves taking in people for weeks, even months. To a German student who wanted to improve her English we gave room and board in
exchange for some help with Anne and Matthew when they were small.
One summer a Brown student lived with us while he worked for a
political candidate we supported. For a year or so we rented a room to a
poor and rather helpless young woman recovering from Hodgkin's
Disease.

These were all, in a sense, transients, however: people with lives of
their own, welcome as sojourners to whatever encouragement and companionship we had to offer until they chose to move elsewhere. At
Chazen, we found people without the power—legal, moral, emotional—to make any such choice. They might leave, if anyone were
willing to take them (many were wards of the state, which meant that

their families, if they had any, were either unwilling or unable to take them), but they'd likely be back, to this place or one like it, until they were old enough to be sent to prison. In light of these realities, we were probably destined, from the moment George started teaching there, to try to rescue at least one of the dozens of children he watched come and go and come.

That one was Ron, but how he came to be Ron and not some other I don't remember. He spent one weekend with us, then another, and another, and gradually a ritual evolved wherein George, who was by now teaching at another school, would drive every Friday afternoon out to Chazen to get him. (The school was located in an area, remote at that time, of the Tucson Mountain foothills, and thus needed no barbed wire. Runaways simply had their shoes taken away. But even faced with acres of rocky ground, cholla and saguaro and prickly pear, rattlesnakes, scorpions, a good many of them went "over the hill.") Friday night, Saturday, Saturday night, Sunday, Ron would spend stretched out in front of the television; often he slept right where he lay, though we had a bed for him in the study. Each Sunday night George would drive him back.

At Christmas that year, 1973 it must have been, he told us he was going home for good. His father hadn't actually said so, but he had sent him a plane ticket, and Ron was sure that once he was home, his father would want him to stay. We had him to our house for an early Christmas before taking him to the airport. I don't recall now just what we gave him—clothes, I think, because he was bursting out of the few articles he owned—but I do remember that after opening his gifts, he disappeared. I found him in the back yard, in the dark, crying softly. "You shouldn't have given me anything," he blurted as I put my arms around him. "I don't have anything for you." "Oh, Ron," I told him, "we don't care. You don't have to give us anything for us to love you." He quieted, but I think now that he didn't believe me. Even after he'd lived with us for a couple of years, he didn't understand why we'd taken him in. "Why do you want me?" he shouted through his tears during one of our rare but agonizing fights. "We love you" was never answer enough. In a life in which survival is based on barter, love can be a pitifully small coin.

Shortly after New Year's, the telephone rang. "I'm at the airport," Ron told George. "Can you come get me?" Despite our hopes, George and I were not surprised, although we didn't tell Ron so. What we did tell him was that when he felt ready to leave the Chazen Institute, he was welcome to live with us. We had to tell him that. Clearly his father wasn't about to take him. And the longer he stayed at Chazen, the more dangerous the lessons he learned. He'd been sent there in the first place for truancy, and already while there he'd been busted for shoplifting a carton of cigarettes. Too, because the system of behavior modification used by the school was teaching him that the only real power he had was the power of manipulating the wielders of the system, he spent increasing amounts of his energy gauging what he could or couldn't get away with. He was a shy sad abandoned child, grieving for his dead mother, tossed out by his father and his new stepmother, growing steadily more sullen and grim and unattractive. We had no idea whether he could survive with us, but plainly he wasn't likely to survive without us.

He took a long time to say yes. I don't mean moments or days. I mean months. During that time he continued to live with us on weekends. In the summer we took him East with us for several weeks as we visited friends and relations. People were polite, but they obviously considered us more than a little gaga: First we'd moved so far west we'd practically dropped off the edge of the earth, and now we reappeared towing this grubby, gawky figure, with neither impeccable genes nor impeccable jeans, his straight black hair to his shoulders and a gold hoop in one ear, who almost never spoke and never, never smiled. Ron, in turn, was faced with a complicated itinerary among clusters of a large and somewhat bumptious family none of whom he could see clearly, his glasses having broken just before the trip. Had we been testing his mettle by this ordeal, he'd have passed with colors soaring.

At the end of the summer he came to stay.

And it was awful. Let there be no doubt about that. Lest anyone be tempted to sentimentalize the situation (and many have), to exclaim about our generosity in taking him in or his good fortune in being taken in, I must make clear that much of what followed was painful and maddening and exhausting for all of us. George and I were faced with sole and full responsibility for a troubled fifteen-year-old in whose upbringing we had had no hand, whose values and attitudes were alien to us, whom, all in all, we could love all right but didn't much like. Anne and Matthew, then nine and five, were faced with a jealous big brother who tormented them in ways limited only by his imagination, which luckily wasn't very resourceful. And Ron was faced with an established family, whose rituals and demands were often beyond him, and whose motives for incorporating him remained obscure and baffling.

The first demand that we made of him was that he stop watching television, and it was very nearly a killer. I find the noise of a television unbearably irritating—after a while it drives me to clenched teeth and tears—and I might have been able to survive his weekends silently weeping and gnashing, but I was never going to make it seven days a week. Anyway, like many parents, George and I worry about the effects of television, and so Anne and Matthew had grown up with restrictions on weekday viewing: PBS from four to six o'clock, special shows by petition. Cooperatively, our elderly black-and-white set blew a tube the day Ron moved in, and George was leisurely in replacing it. He took about a month, if I remember correctly. During that time Ron spent most of his hours out of school lying on his back on his bed, staring at the blank ceiling as though to will on it images of Gomer Pyle. The rest of us read books and magazines. Before that month was out, Ron had started to pick up books and magazines too, and although he returned to the television every permissible hour once it was mended, logging hours of *Sesame Street* and *The Electric Company,* which may have given him some much-needed skills, as well as the grisly collection of Saturday-morning cartoons, he usually spent some part of each day reading as well.

His lack of basic skills worried us a good deal. One day as we were driving along Speedway Boulevard, surely one of the most hideously commercial main thoroughfares in the country, we realized that he could not read most of the signs we were passing but was identifying the stores and restaurants by appearance and logos. Neither George nor I had ever known anyone except tiny children who couldn't read, and we were dismayed. A psychologist at Chazen had told us that although Ron's tests revealed average intelligence, his emotional problems would probably keep him from realizing his full abilities. But at least, we thought, he had got to be able to read. Functional literacy took on lively meaning for us. We began to set him tasks we thought would give him survival skills in a literate society. When we traveled, he read the maps and gave directions, and we never got hopelessly lost. We encouraged him to use the bus system, figuring out times and connections. We ate everything he cooked for us except the batch of brownies for which he misread one-half teaspoon as one-half cup of baking soda; those

45

heaved and crawled up the sides of the pan and all over the oven and were thereby lost to us.

His schooling helped some, of course. We sent him to the Catholic high school of not quite a thousand students where George and I were teaching, in the hope that the atmosphere there would be less daunting than that at the public high school, about three times Salpointe's size, to which he would have been assigned. He had, after all, been incarcerated for truancy, and school obviously held for him terrors that we didn't know but certainly believed. In his two years at Salpointe, he missed two half-days, both with my permission. And although his ability to read and write and figure was still marginal when he graduated, it was at least sufficient to satisfy the Navy.

In many ways, his lack of social skills was more troubling than his lack of academic skills. He had no idea how to form and sustain relationships either within the family or without. Over time, as we began to piece together from various sources the details of his history, we began to understand why he was able neither to give nor to receive the ordinary gestures of human warmth and attachment. What we learned took us well beyond our experiential and conceptual boundaries.

According to a letter from a woman, located by our lawyer as she tried to trace Ron's origins to satisfy guardianship requirements, little "Roddy" was born on 1 October 1958 in Fort Yukon, Alaska, the illegitimate child of an American soldier and an Athabaskan woman. The Athabaskan woman, married with several children already, took him home, but after about a year the tribe told her that she could no longer keep him because he was too white. She took him, hungry and covered with sores, to the woman, who agreed to keep him; but when he was about four, she and her husband divorced. She then gave him to friends who had no children of their own. How accurate this information is we don't know, since we have copies of both a baptismal certificate from St. Stephen's Episcopal Church in Fort Yukon for Elwood Roderick Gabriel, dated 23 November 1958, and a certificate of live birth, dated 3 October 1958, of Elwood Roderick Rose.

At any rate, the couple took him in and renamed him Ronald William DuGay, according to a copy of a baptismal certificate dated 3 July 1962. They raised him, and eventually the man legally adopted him, though not until 8 November 1973. Some time before, his wife had died of some neurological disease. Within six months, he had remarried, a woman with a teen-aged son of her own, who wanted nothing to do with Ron; and so Ron was made a ward of the state of Colorado and sent to Chazen (whose stiff fees were paid for by the federal government since the man was an Army veteran) for refusing to go to school. While Ron was there, we discovered in the elaborate course of obtaining guardianship, which required the man's permission, he moved from Colorado to California without leaving a forwarding address. The sum of these events was a sharp message: Don't settle in too deep, don't put out tendrils of affection: The tendrils will be hacked away: Whoever you love will leave you. I have said that Ron had some learning difficulties, but he was not stupid. He learned this lesson by heart.

Our relationship with Ron's father, whom we never met, was complicated and bitter. I had forgotten, in fact, just how painful it was until I dug out Ron's file and old furies flew out of the folder and gripped me in talons amazingly sharp for all their age. Once we had tracked him down, the man was glad enough to sign the guardianship papers, a legal necessity in case Ron ever needed emergency medical care. Indeed, clearly he wanted to be quit of Ron altogether. He refused to support Ron, or even to send him the few possessions—a bicycle, a Boy Scout backpack and mess kit, an old pony bridle—that Ron had laid up. To get these I used, in one of the ugliest machinations of my life, the only leverage I knew I had: "Unless Ron's things are in his possession by Thanksgiving," I wrote him, "we will return Ron to you. . . . If you will not *share* the responsibility for your son with us, then you must assume *full* responsibility for him." They arrived by Greyhound within a week.

The issue of support was not so readily resolved. Both teachers, George and I made too little money to enable us to take on another mouth to feed, another frame to clothe, especially one that ate and grew prodigiously. But because the man was not an Arizona resident, we could not be paid foster parents under the Arizona Department of Economic Security. The authorities in California rejected a reciprocal agreement, though they would have supported Ron in a foster home in their own state. Our point was not just to get Ron foster care, however; it was to care for him in our own family. At one point the man agreed to send us twenty-two dollars a month, but after two months the checks stopped. Finally, the Veterans Administration arranged garnishment of twenty-five dollars a month from his retirement check, and we had to make do with that. Ron always had enough to eat, I think, but he had few clothes, and with five dollars a week for allowance he could afford few indulgences.

Ron's father may not have been very much to blame in his negligence. He was, according to one of his daughters by his first marriage, a "weak" man who had to have a woman to lean on, and so she was not surprised that he remarried precipitously without caring whether his new wife and Ron could get along. Anyway, I think Ron had been pretty much his mother's child, and she was dead. The man's intelligence and education seemed limited, and he certainly knew nothing of child psychology: It seems never to have occurred to him that Ron's behavior was connected to what was going on in his life. Too, he was aging, with a heart condition; all he wanted was peace and ease. And Ron, smoldering with grief, resentment, rage, was a difficult and threatening presence. I know. I lived with him.

The people who suffered most immediately from that presence were Anne and Matthew. He resented them, of course: They were the "real" children, whose places in the family could never be doubted, whereas he was among us by sufferance, in a position more tenuous in his perception than in actuality. We did not want to get rid of him, but nothing in his experience had taught him that human ties could be so tenacious. I think he always lived on the edge of expulsion. Nothing had taught him gentleness either. The only words he knew to reach the children were threat—"I'm gonna break your arm"—and the only touch a swat, a pinch, the quick wrench of a limb, the yank at a lock of hair. One night he so menaced Matthew that Matthew, in flight, smashed one arm through a glass door, severing the ulnar artery and two tendons.

We were asking a lot of two quite young children. Today I wonder whether we asked too much. The scar on Matthew's wrist is, after seven years, a thin silvery thread. But are there other scars, I wonder, elsewhere than in the flesh, puckers in mind, in emotions, from those years of living with an almost aimless meanness? When I ask the children their feelings about the time Ron lived with us, Matthew's memories are fond, Anne's bitter. Matthew is glad Ron was there, he says—Ron was "fun." Anne makes the kind of face I have learned to associate with her refusal to express strong anger openly. "Do you wish he hadn't come to live with us?" I ask. "I was so young," Matthew explains, "that it never occurred to me that Ron wasn't just part of the family." "And I," says Anne, "was used to beating up on Matthew but not to getting beaten up

on myself." We laugh at this discovery of different perceptions according to place in the family. Matthew, at the bottom of the pecking order
anyway, seems to have figured that Ron's bullying was just part of family life; for Anne he shifted the entire familial structure. She punished
him cruelly for his intrusion, though she looks surprised now when I
tell her so. Far brighter and more self-assured than he, she outwitted
him at turn after turn, jeered at his mistakes in reading, pronunciation,
and simple math, lashed him verbally. Many of his pinches and slaps
may have been retaliatory, as a bear swats at the bees that sting his ears
and nose when he raids their honey. Matthew, with the lovely warmth
he has had since he was a toddler, overwhelmed him in quite another
way: He forgave Ron every blow, every trick, and loved him relentlessly, mean spirit and all.

From Ron's point of view, life in our family must have been a sore
trial. We were told by his counselor at Chazen that he needed a firmly
structured environment, but even without such a caution, the need
would have been clear. He was the most passive child I have ever
known—emotionally, intellectually, even physically inert. When he
stood and walked, his small bony frame seemed to be melting; whenever he could, he lay limply on his bed or in a chair. He could not think
of things to do, even to amuse himself; he lay still for hours, as though
waiting for something to happen to him. He rarely laughed, and then—
a quick bark—only if someone were hurt or humiliated in some way.
Nor did he cry as a rule, or complain, or rebel. He was the only student
George had known at Chazen who never once tried to run away. He was
unnervingly tractable. He would do whatever one demanded. Of course
he would do it as quickly and badly as he could get away with, but so
will most children; his carelessness was, in an odd way, a healthy sign.
His pliancy was scary. The firm structure we were advised to give him
seemed necessary literally to give him a form, keep him intact, so that
he wouldn't dissolve and ooze away.

And so we were strict in our requirements and regulations. Ron had
to attend school every day and a counseling session once a week. He
had to do enough work in his classes to enable him to pass. His fixed
household chores were to wash the dishes and to keep his room decent,
though not necessarily spotless; in addition, we expected him to pitch
in for routine cleaning, shopping, and yard work. If he went out, as he
too seldom did, he had to tell us where he was going and when he'd be
back. Phone calls were limited to fifteen minutes, though often, after

49

he'd begun to make friends, he trotted to the nearest pay phone and chatted to his adolescent heart's content. He was not to drink alcohol, smoke dope, or take anything that didn't belong to him; on these points we were adamant, knowing that, with his record, he could be whisked at the slightest infraction into the juvenile-detention system and we would be helpless to keep him. Anne and Matthew must meet a nearly identical set of demands now that they are teenagers—we didn't create them especially for Ron—but Anne and Matthew have grown up with our expectations, under our discipline. For Ron, adapting to them, suddenly and wholesale, must have been a harsh and often bewildering task.

Living closely with him, we could not always tell whether he was making progress. But gradually he was. His first quarter at Salpointe he was enrolled in the physical education course required for graduation. He had, it turned out, some sort of hang-up about PE, the nature of which we never discovered, though we gathered that it was partly responsible for his earlier truancy. At mid-quarter we received notice that Ron was failing PE because he had never attended. Confronted with the failure warning, he acknowledged that he had just gone off and sat under a tree every day during first period.

"What did you think would happen when we found out?" we asked him.

"I thought I'd get to the mail first," he said.

"But we'd still have found out at the end of the quarter."

He seemed nonplussed. He probably hadn't thought that far ahead. He was even more nonplussed when we told him he'd simply have to take PE another time. Evidently he believed that by his failure he'd cleared himself of the obligation somehow. Quarter after quarter he put it off, waiting, I suppose, for some sign of our relenting. In the last quarter of his senior year, dressing out with a flock of freshmen and sophomores, he took PE, and passed it. He passed all his other courses as well, though perhaps he shouldn't have. We refused to teach him ourselves, but his teachers were our friends in this small, intimate faculty, and they may have been more kind than honest. He made a few friends, and began to wander off campus at lunch to sneak cigarettes and "fool around." He even got hauled into the deans' office one day for getting into a fight. Our bony lump, who had never dared take on anything bigger than a ten-year-old girl, lashed out at another boy just before religion class. We could not condone the act, but we rejoiced in the energy behind it.

As Ron's senior year waned, we grew increasingly worried about his future. Clearly he was going to graduate, with only marginal skills and even poorer initiative. He didn't seem capable of college-level work, even at our local community college. And although one of our demands when he came to live with us had been that he get a part-time job, he had never done so; he claimed to have tried, but we doubted that he had ever screwed his courage so far as to request and fill out an application. He seemed an unlikely candidate for success in the tightening job market. But we would not keep him, we were sure. We were still financially distressed; Anne was old enough to need a room of her own instead of sharing one with Matthew; most of all, we were exhausted. At least by the time he was eighteen, Ron would have to go off on his own.

We were rescued in the most ironic way possible. Ron was incapable of independent action, but he would do as he was told. He needed, then, a situation in which every aspect of his life and work would be regulated. Holy orders offered one alternative, but on the basis of his overweening interest in girls, he did not seem in the least cut out to be a priest. The second most paternalistic organization we could think of after the Catholic church was the military. Two pacifists, radicalized by the grinding ugliness of Vietnam, George and I found ourselves recruiting our foster son for Uncle Sam. His father had been in the Army, of course, and Ron would not, even fleetingly, consider enlistment in the same branch of the service; by this time his fury at his betrayal by his father was flinty. But George had been a naval officer for three years in the early sixties, and George was apparently—though Ron could probably not have said so—okay. Ron took himself to the Naval Recruitment Office, passed the tests, signed the papers. We were all free.

Or almost. We had tried to teach Ron to be scrupulous. Soon after he came to live with us, while we were waiting in line one day at McDonald's, Ron showed me a pair of sunglasses he had lifted from a nearby Circle K. Why is it that children choose to administer these tests in the agora, while you are trying to order three Big Macs and two Quarter-Pounders, two Cokes, a Dr. Pepper, a root beer, and a Sprite, and no thank you, you wouldn't like some hot apple turnovers for dessert, with walls of polyestered shoulders on every side and your five-year-old unloading an entire napkin-holder just beyond your clutching fingers? I told Ron quietly but, I hoped, emphatically that he was not to take things that didn't belong to him, because shoplifting was against the law and we would lose him if he were caught, and that he was to return the sunglasses to the Circle K. I don't know whether he did, but I never

51

saw them again. Nor did I see evidence of other booty, though he was painfully poor compared to most of his classmates and may have succumbed to temptation, especially with regard to a turquoise ring I had given to George which disappeared without a trace. We were equally strict about truthfulness, and I remember him blazing with anger once when I lied to the telephone company, telling them I didn't have an illicit extension phone, to save myself some embarrassment. He accused me of being no better than he had been when he tried to cover up his failure in PE; and he was right. How often our children keep us honest. So it was not surprising that, when the Navy recruiter asked him whether he had ever smoked marijuana, he said that he had. There was a six-month waiting period after the last incident, he was told, and so he could not go into the Navy in August as planned but would have to wait till October.

I nearly wept when I heard of the delay. I was tired—I had just finished a difficult school year, I had not been rehired, the summer heat that aggravates multiple sclerosis symptoms was in full force—and one of the things I was tired of was Ron's presence, especially his ceaseless bickering with the children. And now I was faced with two extra months of it. But as I look back, I'm glad he had the extra time. He still claimed that he couldn't find a job, but once he had graduated I was no longer willing to let the matter slide. He was now, I told him, an adult, and adults had to assume responsibility in society; if he couldn't find a paid job, he'd have to do volunteer work. So he spent several months at the Red Cross, lugging bags of blood about twenty hours each week, and the people there seemed to think well of him. He needed that success. Also, Anne had been promised her own room for her eleventh birthday in September; rather than renege, we simply moved Ron in with Matthew, freeing his room to be redecorated for Anne. Ron was rather nice about his own space and possessions, and I think he began to be eager to escape Matthew's miasma. By the end of the summer, too, his friends had drifted away, into college or jobs. Without the familiar structure of high school, without his own room, without old friends or any way to make new ones, he could look forward to the Navy with some enthusiasm.

Shortly after his eighteenth birthday, we put him on a Greyhound for basic training in San Diego, a skinny, slouching, silent young man with shaggy dark hair and dark-framed glasses, wearing jeans and an open-necked shirt, though as I recall the earring was gone. I don't know whether he was terrified, but I know that I was. He was, after all, my eldest child, the first one to go off, and he seemed more fragile and vulnerable than either of the others. George and I had tried to make the world solid for him and to give him some of the skills we thought he'd need to survive, but we'd had so little time, and we'd made so many mistakes: Most parents get eighteen years; we'd had, all told, not much more than three. I watched the bus pull out of the station and down the narrow street, and when I couldn't see it any more, I watched the point at which it had disappeared, as though I could fix myself to it somehow and travel with Ron across the desert, over the rubbly mountains, down to the blue sweep of San Diego Harbor where once, on a vacation, we had all gone onto the base and stood under the looming grey ships.

The first separation was short, for he was allowed to come home at Christmas. At the airport we couldn't find him; he had to find us. Who was this man in the shirt and tie, the dark uniform and white cap, black stubble covering his round pink head, almost smiling as we reached out to pull him close, almost hugging us back? He was our Ron, and he wasn't. Already he was different. Quiet, not sullen, but quiet, at ease. He teased the children, not as one child taunting others but as a big brother showing off a bit. He brought us fine presents—I still keep my jewelry in the handsome white case with the red satin lining. He talked to us. And then suddenly he was gone again.

We saw him only once more, the following fall, when he had finished radio school and was on his way to a ship in Norfolk. In May 1978 he called to tell us he'd just gotten married to a girl called Angel. In June 1979 his first son was born: Alexander William Randall DuGay. In August 1980, about to be transferred to Keflavik, Iceland, the three got as far as Waco, Texas, to visit Angel's mother, but they couldn't afford the trip to Tucson and we couldn't afford the trip to Waco. In Keflavik, in October 1980, Christopher Jason Allen DuGay was born. Now George and I had a daughter-in-law and two grandbabies we'd never seen. And then at last this summer, between Keflavik and their new duty station in Key West, they came to us.

How strange to see Ron with his wife and children. In five years he has changed some—filled out, grown self-assured—though not so drastically as he did during that first brief separation. Angel I have come to know and like through her good letters. She is the kind of person I enjoy: alert, thoughtful, an enthusiastic tourist, who loves to read and keeps a journal. I worry about her a good deal because, like

53

me, she is easily depressed, and I think that her life, with two such small children, is difficult just now; but so far her courage hasn't failed. At least while he's on leave, Ron takes turns with her watching the boys, who need surprisingly little watching; I've tried to childproof the house, putting our few fragile treasures out of reach, and the only thing that seems in any danger is Lionel Tigress, the new kitten, whom they plaster with pats and sticky kisses. Ron's involvement seems natural, genuine. Almost immediately the night they arrived, Alex threw up all over the dining room, and while Angel raced him to the bathroom, Ron grabbed a roll of paper towels and started mopping. I know a good many men who'd have sat frozen waiting for some woman—and although Angel was otherwise occupied, Anne and I were both available for duty—to cope with the mess. I liked him a lot then. I liked his calm, his competence.

They act like a family. They are a family. Ron has for the first time in his conscious life his own kin, people whose relationship is clear and unequivocal, who belong to him, to whom he belongs, not by sufferance but by right. And he has brought them home to us—home, here, where we are—because we are part of the family, eight of us under one roof. I sense that he has owned us—really owned us, with that matter-of-fact boldness with which children recognize their parents and their siblings—at last. Us: Grandma, Grandpa, Aunt Anne, Uncle Matthew, to whom Alex and Chris, through their father, now have every claim.

People have asked me often whether I regret taking Ron in, whether I'd do so again if I had it to do over. Hard questions to face, the answers risky to the ways I like to think of myself. Because I did regret taking him in, many times. I lack the largeness of spirit that enables someone like George to transcend daily inconveniences, lapses in behavior, even alien values, and to cherish a person without condition. I often judged Ron harshly, by standards inappropriate to his peculiar situation; I was often grudging of approval and affection; I made him work too hard for the privilege of being my son. He suffered, I'm afraid, for my regrets. And no, I think, I wouldn't do it again, knowing what I now know. But then, I wouldn't have Anne and Matthew again either. Might not even marry George again. Such ventures seem now, in the wisdom of hindsight, to demand a woman of more than my mettle. That's how we get wise, by taking on in ignorance the tasks we would never later dare to do.

No. Yes.

A Letter To Matthew

July 1983

My Dear Child—

Last night Daddy and I watched, on William F. Buckley Jr.'s *Firing Line*, a debate whether women "have it as good as men," and I have been talking to you in my head ever since. Odd not to be able to talk with you in person—I'm not yet used to your absence—but I thought I would put onto paper some of the things I would say if you were here. They are not the sort of things I would say to Mr. Buckley if ever I met him. Mr. Buckley is an elderly man, fixed by his circumstances within a range of experiences so narrow that new ideas and new behaviors cannot squeeze through the boundaries. He is complete as he is. But you are just emerging into young manhood, still fluid, still making the choices that will determine the shape that manhood will take. I, as your mother and as a feminist, hope that the choices you make—you individually and your generation as a whole—will be transformative, that the manhood you develop will be so radically new that the question in Mr. Buckley's debate, smacking as it does of competition for goods and goodness, will no longer have any more meaning than questions like "do pigs have it as good as fiddlehead ferns?" or, more aptly, "do pigs have it as good as pigs?"

In many ways, of course, you've dashed my hopes already. You have, after all, lived for fourteen years in a dangerously patriarchal society, and you have put on much of the purple that Mr. Buckley wears with such aplomb. When I find myself disliking you—and I find myself disliking you with about the same regularity, I imagine, as you find yourself disliking me—I can usually tell that I'm responding to some behavior that I identify as peculiarly "masculine." I dislike your cockiness, for instance. When you first began to work with computers, I remember, you immediately assumed the attitude that you knew all that

55

was worth knowing about computers; when you took up racquetball, right away you set yourself up as a champion. This kind of swaggering strikes me as a very old pattern of masculine behavior (I think of Beowulf and Unferth at Heorot), the boast designed to establish superiority and domination, which trigger challenge and thus conflict. Related to your cockiness is your quickness to generalize and, from your generalizations, to pronounce judgments: Calculus is a waste of time; Christians are stupidly superstitious; classical music is boring; Jerry Falwell and the Moral Majority are idiots. This is just the kind of uninformed thinking that empowers Jerry Falwell and the Moral Majority in the first place, of course, this refusal to experience and explore the ambiguities of whatever one is quick to condemn. More seriously, such a pattern of response enables men to create the distinctions between Us and Them—the good guys and the bad guys, the left wing and the right, the Americans and the Russians—that lead to suspicion, fear, hatred, and finally the casting of stones.

Well then, have you shattered *all* my hopes? By no means. For you are not merely arrogant and opinionated. These qualities are overshadowed by another, one I have seldom seen in men: your extraordinary empathic capacity, your willingness to listen for and try to fulfill the needs of others. When Sean was threatening suicide, you were genuinely engaged in his pain. When Katherine needed a male model to encourage her creepy little fifth-grade boys to dance, you leaped in with psychological (if not physical!) grace. When Anne left us for good, I felt your presence supporting and soothing me despite your relief at being an only child at last. Women have long been schooled in this sensitivity to others; but men have been trained to hold themselves aloof, to leave the emotional business of life to their mothers and sisters and wives. I think you are learning to conduct some of that business on your own.

Clearly I believe that the ability to do so is a benefit and not the curse our patriarchal culture has made it out to be. In fact, in an ironic way the answer to Mr. Buckley's question might be that women have it better than men, and it is the fear of such an answer that keeps men nervously posing the question in the first place. You'll remember that Freud ascribed to women a problem he called "penis envy"; a later psychoanalyst, Lacan, called it a "lack." If I've learned anything during the years I've spent in psychotherapy, I've learned that the feelings and motives I ascribe to others tell me little about them but much about myself, for I am projecting my own feelings and motives onto them.

Freud ascribed to women penis envy; ascription = projection; therefore Freud was really suffering from womb envy. QED. A man, lacking the womb and yearning to return to his early identity with the mother, tries to hide his pain by denigrating everything associated with the womb: the blood, the babies, the intuitive and nurturing behaviors of child-rearing. The very condition of having a womb in the first place he labels a pathology: hysteria. If I haven't got it, he tells himself, it can't be worth having. (But maybe, he whispers so softly that even he can't hear, maybe it *is*.)

I'm more than half serious, you know, amid this high-flown silliness. But I don't seriously believe, despite some psychological advantages, that in the "real world" women have it as good as men. In some highly visible ways they have it very bad indeed: They are raped, battered, prostituted, abandoned to raise their children in poverty. Less visibly but no less ruinously, they are brainwashed (often by their mothers and sisters as well as their fathers, brothers, lovers, and husbands) into believing that whatever they get is what they deserve, being only women. Imagine this, Matthew, if you can—and maybe you can, since you are just emerging from childhood, and children are often treated like women in our society. Imagine thinking yourself lucky to get *any* job, no matter how servile or poorly paid, *any* partner, no matter how brutal or dull, *any* roof over your head, no matter how costly the psychic mortgage payment. Imagine believing that's what you deserve. Imagine feeling guilty if you fail to feel grateful.

If you have trouble imagining such conditions, I'm not surprised. I have trouble too; and for many years I held back from calling myself a feminist because I couldn't conceive problems I hadn't experienced. The men in our family do not smack their women and children around. They seldom raise their voices, let alone their palms. They are gentle, courteous, witty, companionable, solicitous. And yet, of late, I've begun to recognize in them certain behaviors and attitudes which suggest that they, too, share a set of cultural assumptions about male power and rights which devalue women's lives. But our men worship their women, you may say; they put them right up on what one of my students once called a "pedastool." True enough, but tell me, how much actual living could you get done confined to a tiny platform several feet above the ground, especially if you had acrophobia?

Look, now that you're staying with them, at Aunt Helen and Uncle Ted, for instance. For forty-eight years they have sustained a relationship founded on domination and submission if ever there was one. Daddy has often insisted that their relationship is fine as long as it works for them. For a long time I tried to accept it too, because I believed that he must be right. I tend, as you know, to believe that Daddy is always right: I'm the product of a patriarchal society too, after all. But now I believe that he's wrong. Although I admire much about their marriage, especially its durability and friendliness, I balk at its basis in a kind of human sacrifice. Trying, I suppose, to compensate for not having graduated from high school, Uncle Ted kept Aunt Helen, a college graduate, confined in a life containing only himself, their one son, and the housework to maintain them. She could have worked, of course—she had the education, and they always needed the money— but Uncle Ted's manly pride insisted on his being the breadwinner, and her job became to stretch the crusts and crumbs from one meager meal to the next. So little had she to occupy her that she grieved for years after her child left for college, and clung to her housework to give her days meaning. Once, in the late sixties, I asked her why she didn't replace her old-fashioned washing machine with an automatic (my mother had had one since 1952), and she replied, "But then what would I do on Mondays?" Worse than the deprivation of stimulating activity has been the undermining of her self-confidence. Even her statements sound like questions, and she repeatedly turns to her husband: "Isn't that right, Ted?" She tiptoes through space as through conversation like our Lionel Tigress, cautious, timorous, whiskers twitching, ready to dash under the bed at a strange voice or a heavy footfall. I like to watch her bake a cake. There in her kitchen she plants her feet firmly and even, sometimes, rattles the pans.

Is Uncle Ted then a monster, some Bluebeard glowering and dangling the incriminating key that represents some independent act that will cost Aunt Helen her head? Hardly. He is a man of sincerity and rectitude, who has lived scrupulously, at considerable cost to himself, according to the code by which he was raised, a code that Rudyard Kipling, whom he admires, described as the "white man's burden." In it, women (among others, such as our "darker brethren") require the kind of protection and control they are unable, being more "natural" creatures, to provide themselves. He adores Aunt Helen, I do believe, and wants to do only what's best for her. But he assumes that he knows what's best for her, and so does she. In the name of manhood, he has taken from her the only authentic power a human being can hold: that of knowing and choosing the good. Such theft of power results in mastery. There is no mistressy.

I've been uneasy, as you know, about your spending this summer with them, largely, I suppose, because I don't want Uncle Ted to make a "man" of you. And I've encouraged you to subvert their patterns of interaction in a small way, by helping Aunt Helen with her chores just as you help Uncle Ted with his, even when he tries to divert you and she tells you to run along with him, not so that you can change those patterns (you can't) but so that you'll remain aware of them. You may well be tempted to fall into them because what Uncle Ted construes as "men's work" is infinitely more interesting than "women's work." You already know what a drag it is to set the table knowing that within an hour the dishes will be streaked and gummy, to wash those dishes knowing that they'll go right back on the table for breakfast, to fold a whole line of clothes that will crawl straight back into the hamper, muddy and limp, to be washed and hung out again. How much more pleasant and heartening to tramp through the woods checking the line from the brook, to ride the lawnmower round and round on the sweet falling grass, to plot traps for porcupines and saw down trees and paddle the canoe across the pond spreading algicide and possibly falling in. If everyone washed the dishes together, of course, everyone could go for a walk in the woods. How one would tell the men from the women, though, I'm not sure.

But then, so what if you do fall into the patterns? Surely the world won't end if you and Uncle Ted take the fishing rods down to the Battenkill to catch a few trout for breakfast, leaving Aunt Helen to make the beds? Well yes, I think in a way it will, and that's why I'm writing you this letter. For Aunt Helen and Uncle Ted's marriage is not in the least extraordinary. On the contrary, the interactions between them, despite some idiosyncracies, are being played out in millions of relationships throughout the world, including, in its own way, Daddy's and mine, within which you have lived your whole life. One partner is telling the other (though seldom in words) that she is weaker physically and intellectually, that her concerns are less meaningful to the world at large, that she is better suited (or even formed by God) to serve his needs in the privacy of his home than to confront the tangled problems of the public sphere. And instead of ignoring his transparent tactics for enhancing his uncertain self-image and increasing his own comfort, she is subordinating her needs to his, accepting the limits he decrees, and thereby bolstering the artificial pride that enables him to believe himself a "superior" creature. As soon as he feels superiority, he is capable of dividing his fellow creatures into Us and Them and of trying to dominate Them. That is, he is ready to make war.

This connection—between the private male who rules his roost and keeps his woman, however lovingly, in her place and the public male who imposes his will by keeping blacks poor and pacifying Vietnamese villages and shipping arms and men to Central America—is far from new. Virginia Woolf made it in *Three Guineas* nearly fifty years ago. "The public and the private worlds are inseparably connected," she wrote; "the tyrannies and servilities of the one are the tyrannies and servilities of the other." But *Three Guineas* has been largely ignored or denigrated: One male critic called it "neurotic," "morbid"; another, "cantankerous." (You know, I am sure, that whan a man speaks out, he is assertive, forthright; when a woman speaks her "mind," she is sick or bitchy.) Moreover, its feminism has been labeled "old-fashioned," as though already in 1938 the problems Woolf named had been solved. If so, why do we stand today in the same spot she stood then, looking at the same photographs of dead bodies and burned villages? No, her feminism isn't out of date, though such a label shows a desperate attempt to set it aside. Rather, it says something, valid today, that men still do not want to hear: that if humanity—men and women —is to have it any good at all, men must give up their pleasure in domination, their belief in their superiority, the adulation of their fellow creatures, at the personal and private level of their lives. Now. They must stop believing that whoever they love will perish without their "protection," for the act of protecting leads to a sense of possession, and it necessitates enemies to protect from. They must completely and radically revise their relationships with themselves, their wives and children, their business associates, the men and women in the next block, the next city, the next country. They must learn to say to every other who enters their lives not, "You're over there, and you're bad," but, "You're over there, and you're me."

Can they do it? Some feminists think not. They say that we should simply kill men off (except perhaps for the babies) and start fresh. I understand the anger that fuels such a proposal and the desire to sweep the rubbishy world clean. But I reject it because it perpetuates the violence that distinguishes masculine solutions to conflict. Our cultural heritage would still be based on killing, our mythology rooted in massacre.

No, I think that I will let you live. Will you let me live? If so, the terms of your existence must be transformed. What's been good enough for Aunt Helen and Uncle Ted, for Mr. Buckley, for Ronald Reagan and the other men who govern us and every other nation, for the Catholic Church, for the medical and legal professions, for the universities, for all the patriarchy, cannot be good enough for you. (And I address you personally, though obviously I mean all young men everywhere, because moral choice is always a lonely matter. You may all encourage one another—in fact, if the transformation is working, you will—but each will have to choose his way of being for himself.) You must learn to develop your identity through exploring the ways you are like, not different from or better than, others. You must learn to experience power through your connections with people, your ability to support their growth, not through weakening them by ridicule or patronage or deprivation. If this means dancing with the little boys, then dance your heart out; they'll dance on into the future with more assurance because of you. And who can shoot straight while he's dancing?

I am demanding something of you that takes more courage than entering a battle: not to enter the battle. I am asking you to say *no* to the values that have defined manhood through the ages—prowess, competition, victory—and to grow into a manhood that has not existed before. If you do, some men and women will ridicule and even despise you. They may call you spineless, possibly even (harshest of curses) womanish. But your life depends on it. My life depends on it. I wish you well.

Now go help Aunt Helen with the dishes.

I love you—
Mother

On Being Raised by a Daughter

Mothering. I didn't know how to do it. Does anyone? If there really were a maternal instinct, as a good many otherwise quite responsible human beings have claimed, then would we need men like Dr. Alan Guttmacher and Dr. Benjamin Spock to teach us how to mother, and would we be forever scrambling to keep up with the shifts in their child-bearing and child-rearing theories? Would we turn, shaken by our sense of our female incapacity, to the reassuring instructive voices of the fathers, who increasingly come in both sexes, murmuring how much weight to gain or lose, how long to offer the breast, how soon to toilet train, to send to school? Does the salmon ask for a map to the spawning ground? Does the bee send to the Department of Agriculture for a manual on honeymaking?

No, I came with no motherly chromosomes to pattern my gestures comfortably. Not only did I not know how to do it, I'm not even sure now that I wanted to do it. These days people choose whether or not to have children. I am not so very old—my forty-first birthday falls this month—yet I can say with the verity of a wrinkled granny that we did things differently in my day. I no more chose to have children than I had chosen to get married. I simply did what I had been raised to do. Right on schedule (or actually a little ahead of schedule, since I hadn't yet finished college) I wrapped myself in yards of white taffeta and put orange blossoms in my hair and marched myself, in front of the fond, approving gaze of a couple of hundred people, into the arms of a boy in a morning coat who was doing what he had been raised to do. After a year or so, the fond, approving gaze shifted to my belly, which I made swell to magnificent proportions before expelling an unpromising scrap of human flesh on whom the gaze could turn. This was Anne, created in a heedless gesture as close to instinctual as any I would ever perform:

satisfaction of the social expectation that I, young, vigorous, equipped with functioning uterus and ovaries and breasts, would sanctify my union with George by bringing forth a son. (I missed, though I had better luck next time.)

The birth of Anne was dreadful, and at the beginning I hated her, briefly, more fiercely than I had ever hated anyone. My doctor, a small round elderly GP who delivered whatever babies came along in Bath, Maine, told me that my protracted pelvis might necessitate a Caesarian section, but he never instructed me what to do during this birth by whatever means. I guess I was supposed not to do but to endure. I remember, hours into a lengthy and complicated labor that ended in Dr. Fichtner's extracting Anne with forceps like a six-pound thirteen-ounce wisdom tooth, twisting my fingers through my hair, yanking, raking my face with my nails, shrieking at the nurse beside me, "Get this thing out of me! I hate it!" Until then I had rather liked Anne, as she humped up bigger and bigger each night under the bedsheet, her wriggles and thumps giving a constant undertone of companionship to my often solitary daily activities. But now I was sure she was killing me. The nurse loosened my fingers and soothed, "You'll feel differently in a little while."

She was right. In a rather long while I did feel differently. I was no longer in pain. But I didn't feel motherly. In fact, Anne on the outside wasn't half so companionable as Anne on the inside, and I think I felt a little lonely. And frightened. I hadn't the faintest idea what I was doing with this mite with the crossed blue eyes and the whoosh of hair sticking straight up. And now, more than eighteen years later, I still have the frequent sense that I don't know what I'm doing, complicated now, of course, by the guilt that I don't know what I've done and the terror that I don't know what I'm going to do. How, I wonder when a young woman comes into my room and speaks to me, her hair blown dry to casual elegance and her eyes uncrossed behind round brown frames, how did you get here? And where, when you turn and walk out of here, out of my house and out of the dailiness of my life, where will you go?

I have been mystified by motherhood largely because motherhood itself has been mystified. Perhaps before Freud I might have raised my children without knowing consciously my power to damage their spirits beyond human repair, but the signs have always been there: the Good Mother and the Terrible Mother; the dead saint and the wicked stepmother waiting to offer disguised poisons, shoes of hellfire. The one is as alien as the other. If you live in a culture where all children are raised by mothers, Nancy Chodorow points out in *The Reproduction of Mothering*, and if half those children are males who must separate with some violence from the mother in order to establish their different gender, and if the males have the power to determine, through the creation of symbolic systems like language and art, what culture itself is, then you will get a cultural view of mothers as others, on whom are projected traits that even they (who speak some form of the language, who look at the pictures even if they don't paint them) come to assume are their own. We live in a culture of object-mothers. The subject-mothers, culturally silenced for millennia, are only just beginning to speak.

The voices of authority tell me I may harm, even ruin my daughter (in large measure by spoiling her for the pleasurable uses of men). At first they issue from the eminences of science, in measured tones like those of Carl Jung: "Thus, if the child of an over-anxious mother regularly dreams that she is a terrifying animal or a witch, these experiences point to a split in the child's psyche that predisposes it to a neurosis." I am the stuff of my daughter's nightmares. Gradually the pronouncements trickle down into the market place and are reformulated for popular consumption by voices like Nancy Friday's in that long whine of sexual anxiety *My Mother/My Self*, which was on the bestseller list some years back: "When mother's silent and threatening disapproval adds dark colors to the girl's emergent sexuality, this fear becomes eroticized in such strange forms as masochism, love of the brute, rape fantasies—the thrill of whatever is most forbidden." I make of my daughter's life a waking nightmare as well. A book like *My Mother/My Self*, in dealing with our earliest relationship, out of which our ability to form all other relationships grows, taps a rich subterranean vein of desire and disappointment, but it does so only to portray daughter as victim.

The real danger these voices pose lies not so much in what they say as in what they leave out about motherhood, whether through ignorance or through incapacity. Jung was not a woman at all, at least socially speaking (archetypally, of course, he had an anima, which doesn't seem to have caused him much trouble). And Friday refused to have children on the grounds that if she chanced to have a daughter, she'd ruin her child just as her mother had ruined her (such an assumption suggests that her choice was a wise one). But neither these two nor the vast crowd of fellow motherhood-mystifiers between them

65

takes into adequate account the persistence of human development, which keeps the personality malleable indefinitely, if it is allowed to, or the implacable power of six pounds thirteen ounces of human flesh from the moment it draws a breath and wails its spirit out into the world.

Among all the uncertainties I have experienced about myself as a mother, of one point I feel sure: that I am not today the woman I would have been had Anne not been born one September evening almost nineteen years ago. I cannot prove this hypothesis, there being no control in this experiment, no twenty-two-year-old Nancy Mairs that night who had a son instead, whose baby died, who had had a miscarriage, who had not been able to get pregnant at all, who never married and lives now in a small, well-appointed apartment on the Marina in San Francisco, walking her Burmese cats on leashes in Golden Gate Park. There is only this Nancy Mairs who, for nearly half her life, has in raising been raised by a daughter.

Anne can't have found her job an easy one. Raising a mother is diffi-cult enough under the best of circumstances. But when you get one who's both crippled and neurotic—who doesn't do her fair share of the housework, who lurches around the house and crashes to the floor in front of your friends, whose spirits flag and crumple unpredictably, who gets attacks of anxiety in the middle of stores and has to be cajoled into finishing simple errands—then you have your work cut out for you. Of all the things Anne has taught me, perhaps the most important is that one can live under difficult circumstances with a remarkable amount of equanimity and good humor. It's a lesson I need daily.

My education began, no doubt, from the moment of her birth. Per-haps even before. Perhaps from the moment I perceived her presence in the absence of my period, or from the instant (Christmas Eve, I'm con-vinced) of her conception, or even from the time I began to dream her. But then she was anonymous. As soon as she appeared, she took me firmly in diminutive hand and trained me much as I've come to see that my cats have trained me, rewarding my good behavior (what difference a smile or a purr?) and punishing my bad (they've both tended to bite). But I don't think of my education as being under way till about nine months later when one day she heaved herself up in her car-bed, raised one arm in a stiff wave, and called, "Hi there!" A baby who could talk with me was beyond my ken. After all, I was raised before the days when dolls had electronic voice-boxes in their tummies and quavered

"Hi there!" when you pulled the string. And anyway, Anne didn't have a string. *She* chose to speak to *me*.

I've never been the same.

Birth is, I think, an attenuated process, though we tend to use the word to describe only the physical separation of the baby from the mother. Fortunately, those first hours of birth were the worst, in terms of pain, or I don't think I'd have lasted. Each phase of the process involves separation, which may or may not be physical but always carries heavy psychic freight. For me, Anne's speech was a major step. It set her apart from me, over there, an entity with whom I could, literally, have a dialogue. It made her an other.

Feminist psychologists note that psychical birth, the process of differentiating self from other, is particularly problematic for female children. As Chodorow writes,

> Because they are the same gender as their daughters and have been girls, mothers of daughters tend not to experience these infant daughters as separate from them in the same way as do mothers of infant sons. . . . Primary identification and symbiosis with daughters tend to be stronger and cathexis of daughters is more likely to retain and emphasize narcissistic elements, that is, to be based on experiencing a daughter as an extension or double of a mother herself, with cathexis of the daughter as a sexual other usually remaining a weaker, less significant theme.

The consequence of this feeling of continuity between mother and daughter is that "separation and individuation remain particularly female developmental issues." But "problematic" doesn't mean "bad," a leap that Friday makes when she lifts "symbiosis" out of the psychoanalytic context in which Chodorow uses it and applies it to noninfantile relationships, giving it then not its full range of meaning but that portion of meaning which suits her program: symbiosis as a kind of perverse parasitism: a large but weak organism feeding on a smaller but strong host which, as it grows, weakens until the two are evenly matched in size and incapacity. According to Friday, the mother limits her daughter's autonomy and independence, extinguishes her sexuality, terrifies her witless of men, then packages her in Saran Wrap to keep her fresh and hands her over to some man who, if she's not careful, will get on her a daughter on whom she will perform the same hideous rites.

I'm not saying that no mother does such things. Apparently Nancy Friday's mother did, and I recognize any number of my own experi-

67

ences in hers. Nor am I saying that, through some virtue or miracle, I have avoided doing them to Anne. Of course I would want to think so; but God and Anne alone know what horrors I've perpetrated. All I can be sure of is that if Anne handed me a list of grievances, most of them would probably surprise me. If they didn't, I'd be a monster, not a mother.

What I am saying is that such things are not intrinsic to the mother-daughter relationship. As Chodorow notes in her study "Family Structure and Female Personality," women in societies as various as those in Atjeh, Java, and East London, where their "kin role, and in particular the mother role, is central and positively valued," have experiences and develop self-images very different from those of Western middle-class women:

> There is another important aspect of the situation in these societies. The continuing structural and practical importance of the mother-daughter tie not only ensures that a daughter develops a positive personal and role identification with her mother, but also requires that the close psychological tie between mother and daughter become firmly grounded in real role expectations. These provide a certain constraint and limitation upon the relationship, as well as an avenue for its expression through common spheres of interest based in the external social world.

Thus, although the problem of differentiation exists wherever mothers mother daughters, its implications vary from one social setting to another. If a woman like Friday's mother teaches her daughter that sex is risky at best and in general downright nasty, she does so not because she is a mother but because she is the product of a patriarchal order that demands that its women be chaste and compliant so that men may be sure of their paternity. In fact, such a concern is extrinsic to the mother-daughter relationship, which exists in essence outside the sphere of men. As soon as one can identify it for what it is, the concern of a particular group of human beings for maintaining a particular kind of power, one is free to choose whether or not to perpetuate it.

Thus, Friday's rationale for refusing to bear children, that she would inevitably visit upon her daughter the same evils her mother visited upon her, is off the mark, rooted in a sense of powerlessness in the face of the existing social order which seems to stem from belief in a biologically predetermined parasitism. Mothers, inexorably, must eat out the hearts of their daughters alive. Neither a mother nor a daughter has the power to avoid the dreadful outcome. They are only helpless women. But if we step outside socially imposed injunctions, then Friday is wrong, and daughters and their mothers wield powers for one another's help as well as harm. They may even make of one another revolutionaries.

Symbiosis is a spacious word. It may encompass parasitism and helotism (though the *Shorter Oxford Dictionary* disallows this meaning by requiring that the entities involved be mutually supportive). But it also—even chiefly—means commensalism, mutualism, "the intimate living together," says *Webster's Third*, "of two dissimilar organisms in any of various mutually beneficial relationships." The crux is the living-withness the word demands: We may live with one another well or badly. To live together reciprocally, each contributing to the other's support, in the figurative sense in which symbiosis represents human relationship, requires delicate balance, difficult to establish and to maintain. Both partners must give to it and take from it. Both must flourish under its influence, or it is no longer symbiotic. For these reasons, a symbiotic relationship between a mother and her growing daughter—or between any other two people, for that matter—may be rather rare. For these reasons, also, emotional symbiosis is not an ascribed characteristic of a relationship; rather, it is the outcome of the dynamics of some relationships between some people some of the time.

Symbiosis as I am now using the word—not like Chodorow to represent the phase of total infantile dependence or like Friday to suggest emotional vampirism but rather as a metaphor for the interdependence characteristic of living together well—does not result in identity. On the contrary, every definition I've found requires the difference of the entities involved. Thus, after the demands of infancy have been made and met, individuation is necessary if a true symbiotic system is to be maintained. Otherwise you get something else, some solid lump of psychic flesh whose name I do not know.

All the analyses I've read of mother-daughter relationships fail to account for my experience of Anne's power in our mutual life. The assumption seems to be that I'm the one in control, not just because I'm older than she is and, until recently, bigger and stronger, but because I have society's acknowledgment and support in the venture and she doesn't. I'm engaged in the honorable occupation of child-rearing, and if I can't figure the procedures out for myself, I can find shelves of manuals in any bookstore or library. No one even notices that Anne is engaged in mother-rearing, much less offers her any hot tips; indeed, books like *My Mother/My Self* only reinforce her powerlessness, making her out a victim of maternal solicitude and submerged rage, whose only recourse is more rage, rebellion, rejection: not an actor but a reactor. Such lopsided accounts arise, I suppose, from the premise—the consequence of a hierarchical view of human development—that adulthood signifies completion. But the fluidity, the pains and delights, the spurts of growth and sluggish spells of childhood never cease, though we may cease to acknowledge them in an effort to establish difference from, and hence authority over, our children. Out of the new arrivals in our lives—the odd word stumbled upon in a difficult text, the handsome black stranger who bursts in one night through the cat door, the telephone call out of a friend's silence of years, the sudden greeting from the girl-child—we constantly make of ourselves our selves.

When Anne waved and called out to me, she made an other not only of herself but of me. Language is the ultimate alienator. When she spoke she created for herself a self so remote from me that it could communicate with me only—imprecisely, imperfectly—through words. Shortly thereafter she named me, and went on naming me, into place, a slowish process. When she was not quite two, I left the world. I went into a state mental hospital and stayed there six months. During that time Anne lived with my mother, another Anne, and the two of them built a life around a space that they both expected me to come back to and fill. One afternoon, sitting in a basket in the checkout line at the IGA, Anne struck up a conversation with the man behind her who, gesturing toward Mother, said something about her mummy. "That's not my Mummy," Anne informed him, drawing herself high and fixing him with one crossed eye. "It's my Grandma. My Mummy is in the hospital." When Mother told me this story, I heard the message as I've heard it ever since: I'm the Mummy, the only Mummy (though I've grown up to be Mom, that hearty jokey apple-pie name, for reasons known only to my children), and that's who I've got to be.

As Mummy I have emphatically never been permitted to be Anne. Whatever fantasies I may have had, at some subliminal level, of my new daughter as a waxen dolly that I could pinch and pat into my likeness, Anne scotched them early, probably when she first spat puréed liver into my face (not to mention when she became the only one in the family who today eats liver in any form), certainly by the time she shouted out "Hi there!" (not "Mama" or "Dada," no private communiqué, but a greeting to all the world). Nor can I ever make her me. She wouldn't let me. Hence the possibility for our symbiosis, a state that demands two creatures for its establishment and mainte-nance. Anne has schooled me in the art of living well together by letting go.

Like any daughter's, hers hasn't been a simple task, but I don't think that the kind of gritty spirit it's called up in her will stand her in bad stead. She has been hampered by my own terror of separation, brought on perhaps by my early separation from my mother because of illness or my somewhat later permanent separation from my father through death. She has been helped, I think, by my curiosity to see what she would do next and by the fact that I've worked at jobs I enjoy since she was nine months old and that I've remained married, in considerable contentment, to her father, for as Chodorow points out, when "women do meaningful productive work, have ongoing adult companionship while they are parenting, and have satisfying emotional relationships with other adults, they are less likely to overinvest in children." And at least I've always *wanted* to let go. I just haven't always known how or when. Anne, through her peculiar quiet stubborn self-determination, has time after time peeled my white-knuckled fingers loose and shrugged away from my grasp.

Neither of us has had a whole lot of help from the world at large. We live in a society that still expects, even demands, that mothers control and manipulate their children's actions right into adulthood; that judges them according to the acceptability or unacceptability of their children's appearance and behavior; and that ensures their dependence on maternity for a sense, however diffuse, of self by giving them pre-cious little else of interest to do. The mother who does let go, especially of a daughter, is still often considered irresponsible at best, unnatural at worst.

When Anne was sixteen, for instance, she decided to join a volunteer organization called Amigos de las Americas, training in Spanish and public health for several months and then going to Honduras to vacci-nate pigs against hog cholera. United States policies in Central America hadn't yet created thoroughgoing chaos, and George and I thought this a wonderful way for her to begin inserting herself into the world. But George's parents, on a visit during her preparations, challenged me about Anne's plans. She ought not to be allowed to go, they said. It would be too much for her. The shock of entering a new culture would make her emotionally ill. "Ugh," Mum Mairs shuddered, "girls

71

shouldn't have to dig latrines." (At that time, Anne hadn't yet received her assignment, but I presume that girls shouldn't have to slog around in pigshit either.) I was so startled by this attack, in terms I had not thought of before, that I doubt I said much to allay their fears, though I did ask Anne to tell them about her training in order to reassure them that she wasn't being thrust into the jungle naked and naive. Meanwhile, I thought about those terms, those feminine terms, forgotten at least momentarily by me, foreign as a source of motivation to Anne: nicety, physical and emotional frailty, passivity: all rolled into that statement that girls shouldn't have to dig latrines. (The logical extension of this attitude, I suppose, is that if a girl is all you've got, then you don't get a latrine. Ugh.)

Later, comparing notes with George, I learned that his parents had never mentioned the matter to him. I was at first hurt, angry, feeling picked on; later I came to understand that I was the natural target of their misgivings. George couldn't be counted on to know what girls should or shouldn't do, or to communicate his knowledge if he did. But I could. I was Anne's mother. And in letting her go to Latin America to live, if only briefly, in poverty, perhaps in squalor, and to perform manual labor, I was derelict in my duty.

Thus challenged, I had to rethink this duty. To Mum and Dad Mairs, obviously, it entailed the same protection I received growing up: keeping Anne safe and comfortable, even keeping her pure, at bottom probably protecting her maidenhead, though this mission is buried so deep in our cultural unconscious that I think they would be shocked at the mention of it. I recognized a different duty, a harsher one: to promote Anne's intellectual and spiritual growth even if it meant her leaving me. I didn't think that safety and comfort tended to lead to growth. As for protecting her maidenhead, I figured that was her responsibility, since she was the one who had it, or didn't have it, as the case might be. My duty, I saw, might in fact *be* dereliction, in the form of releasing her into the flood of choice and chance that would be her life. I thought she could swim. More important, she thought she could swim. Nonetheless, while she was gone I ran around distracted and stricken with guilt, mumbling primitive prayers to Our Lady of Guadalupe to take up the watch I had left off. Then she came home, bearing rum and machetes wide-eyed right through customs, with a new taste for mangoes and a new delight in hot showers but without even the lice and dysentery and other gruesome manifestations of tropical fauna she had been promised.

She came back but never, of course, all the way back. Each departure contains an irrevocable element of private growth and self-sufficiency. For the most part I have thought her departures thrilling: the month she spent in New England with her grandparents when she was eight, flying back to Tucson alone; her first period; the first night she spent (quite chastely) with a boy, and later her first lover; her excellence at calculus; her choice to leave lover and family and lifelong friends to go to college on the other side of the country. As long as her new flights give her joy, I rejoice. Where I balk—and balk badly—is at those junctures where the growing hurts her.

One night a couple of winters ago, I woke from heavy early sleep to a young man standing in the dark by my bed: David, Anne's boyfriend. "Mrs. Mairs," he whispered, "I think you'd better come. Anne is drunk and she's really sick and I think you should take care of her." Clearly David wasn't drunk, hadn't been at the same party, he explained, but had met up with Anne afterward. He'd taken her to a friend's house, and though Chris wasn't at home, his mother had kindly taken them in, given them some tea, let Anne throw up in her toilet. But it was getting late, and David had a deadline. He had to bring Anne home, but he didn't dare leave her alone.

I hauled myself out of bed and padded to the other end of the cold house, where Anne was in her bathroom washing her face. When she heard my voice, she hissed, "David, I'll kill you," then came out and burst into tears. I sent David along as I held and rocked her, listening to her wretched tale. She certainly was drunk. The fumes rising from my sodden lap were enough to make me tiddly. Gradually I got her quieted and tucked into bed. The next day she felt suitably miserable. To this day she prefers milk to alcohol.

The children were surprised that I wasn't angry about this episode. In a way I was surprised myself. After all, I had forbidden Anne to drink alcohol outside our house, and she had disobeyed me. Wasn't anger the appropriate response to a disobedient child? But though I specialize in appropriate responses, I did not feel angry. Instead, I felt overwhelmingly sad. For days I was stabbed to the heart by the thought of Anne reeling and stumbling along a darkened street, her emotions black and muddled, abandoned by the group of nasty little boys who had given her beer and vodka and then gone off to have some other fun.

By that one act she stripped me of whatever vestiges of magical thinking I was clinging to about mothers and daughters. Until then, I think, I had still believed that through my wisdom and love I could

73

protect her from the pains I had endured as a child. Suddenly my shield was in tatters. It was a thing of gauze and tissue anyway. She has taught me the bitterest lesson in child-rearing I've yet had to learn: that she will have pain, must have it if she is to get to—and through—this place I am now and the places to which I have yet to go. For, as Juliet Mitchell writes, "pain and lack of satisfaction are the point, the triggers that evoke desire," that essential longing which marks our being in the world, both Anne's and mine, as human.

In teaching me to be her mother, Anne has, among all her other gifts, given me my own mother in ways that have often surprised me. For, as the French theorist Julia Kristeva writes in *Desire in Language*, "By giving birth, the woman enters into contact with her mother; she becomes, she is her own mother; they are the same continuity differentiating itself." Old rebellions have softened, old resentments cooled, now that I see my mother stereoscopically, the lens of motherhood superimposed on that of daughterhood. Every child, I'm sure, takes stern and secret vows along these lines: "When I grow up, I'm never going to make my child clean her room every Saturday, wear orange hair ribbons, babysit her sister, eat pea soup. . . "; and every mother must experience those moments of startlement and sometimes horror when she opens her mouth and hears issue forth not her own voice but the voice of her mother. Surprisingly often, I have found, my mother's voice speaks something that I, as a mother, want to say. I can remember that, when I had accepted a date with Fred—squat, chubby, a little loud, a French kisser, the bane of my high-school love life—and then got a better offer, Mother told me I had only two choices, to go with Fred or to stay home. I vowed then that I would never interfere with my child's social life. But I have had occasion to issue the same injunction, not because I can't tell where my mother ends and I begin, nor because I want Anne to suffer the same horrors I endured in the course of becoming a woman, but because I believe that the habit of courtesy toward one's fellow creatures is more durable than a fabulous night at the prom. Mother may have thought so too.

I gave Mother more trouble throughout my years at home than Anne has given me because, through some psychic and/or biochemical aberration, I was a depressive, though neither she nor I knew so at the time. I recognized that my behavior was erratic and that she got very angry with me for it. What I didn't see, and maybe she didn't either, was that behind her anger lay the anxiety and frustration caused by her helplessness to protect me from my pain. When, finally, I cracked up suffi-

74

ciently to be sent to a mental hospital, I sensed that she was blaming herself for my troubledness (and no wonder in the disastrous wake of Freud), and I felt impatient with her for believing such silliness. But she was only exhibiting that reflexive maternal guilt which emerges at the infant's first wail: "I'm sorry. I'm sorry. I'm sorry I pushed you from this warm womb into the arms of strangers, me among them. I'm sorry I can't keep you perfectly full, perfectly dry, perfectly free from gas and fear, perfectly, perfectly happy." Any mother knows that if she could do these things, her infant would die more surely than if she covered its face with a rose-printed pillow. Still, part of her desire is to prevent the replication of desire.

Because I knew I had so often infuriated and wearied her, when I left for college I thought only of Mother's relief, never of the possibility that she might miss me. Why should she? The house was still crammed without me, my sister Sally still there, and my stepfather and the babies, and my grandmother too, not to mention an elderly Irish setter and a marmalade cat. As soon as I'd gone, Mother bought a dishwasher, and I figured that took care of any gap I'd left. Not until Anne began the process of selecting a college, finding a summer job in Wisconsin, packing away her mementoes, filling her suitcases did I think that Mother's first-born daughter (and not just a pair of hands in the dishpan) had once left her, and she must have grieved at the separation too. I love to visit her now because I know at last that she is delighted to have me there — not just glad of the company — but warmed and entertained by *me*, one of the daughters who raised her.

I am aware, too, that she once raised a mother, Granna, who lived with us for many years. And Granna raised a mother, Grandma Virchow, with whom she and Mother lived for many years. And Grandma must have raised a mother as well, left behind in Germany in the 1890s, who must herself have raised a mother. "For we think back through our mothers if we are women," writes Virginia Woolf in *A Room of One's Own*. Anne has helped me in that backward dreaming. When she tells me that she doesn't plan to have children, I feel sad, but not because I won't have grandchildren. I mean, I'd welcome them, but I have quite enough characters populating my life to keep me entertained. Rather, I would like her to have this particular adventure, this becoming that a daughter forces.

Overall, I think Anne has done a pretty good job with me. Even without encouragement, in a society that doesn't consider her task authentic, she's done her share of leaning and hauling, shaping me to her

75

needs, forcing me to learn and practice a role I have often found wearying and frightening. Maybe some women are mothers by nature, needing only an infant in their arms to bloom. I'm not. I've needed a lot of nurture. And still I hate it sometimes, especially when she makes me into an authoritarian ogre rumbling disapproval (just as I did to Mother, oh, how many times?). But she's firm and often fair. She doesn't coddle me. Years ago, before I got my brace, I used to have a lot of trouble putting on my left shoe and she would help me with it; the right shoe she'd hand me, saying, "You can do this one yourself." But on my birthday she bakes me lemon bread and, when I ask her what I smell, tells me she's washing dishes in lemon-scented detergent. I believe her and so am surprised by my birthday party. She is tolerant when I stamp my feet (figuratively speaking—if I really stamped my feet I'd fall in a heap and then we'd both get the giggles) and refuse to let her take my peach-colored gauze shirt to Honduras. But she is severe about suicide attempts. She has no use for my short stories, in which she says nothing ever happens, but she likes my essays, especially the ones she appears in, and sometimes my poems. She admires my clothing (especially my peach-colored gauze shirt), my hair, my cooking, but not my taste in music or in men. When my black cat, Bête Noire, the beast of my heart, was killed, she let me weep, hunched over, my tears splashing on the linoleum, and she never said, "Don't cry."

Before long Anne will have to consider the job done. A daughter can't spend a lifetime raising her mother any more than a mother can spend a lifetime raising her daughter; they both have other work to get on with. I can remember the liberating moment when I recognized that it was no longer my task to educate my mother in the ways of the real world; she'd just have to make the best of what she'd learned and muddle along on her own. Mother muddles well, I like to think because I gave her a good start. Anne deserves such a moment.

And I deserve her having it. It's what we've come this way for. Last summer, when George was visiting his parents, his mother sighed, "Life is never so good after the children have gone." George is her only child, and he's been gone for twenty-five years. I can't imagine sustaining a quarter of a century of anticlimax. Anne and I both confront transformation into women with wholly new sets of adventures as we learn to live well apart. I feel pretty well prepared now for muddling along on my own.

WRITING

On Not Liking Sex

"The other day, sitting in a tweed chair with my knees crossed, drinking a cup of coffee and smoking a cigarette, I looked straight at my therapist and said, 'I don't like sex.' I have known this man for years now. I have told him that I don't like my husband, my children, my parents, my students, my life. I may even have said at some time, 'I don't like sex very much.' But the difference between not liking sex very much and not liking sex is vast, vaster even than the Catholic Church's gulf between salvation and damnation, because there's no limbo, no purgatory. An irony here: For in another age (perhaps in this age within the bosom of the Holy Mother Church) I would be the woman whose price is above rubies, pure and virtuous, purity and virtue having always attached themselves, at least for women, to the matter of sex. As it is, I am, in my metaphor, one of the damned. My therapist has a homelier metaphor. I have, he says, what our society considers 'the worst wart.' In 1981 in the United States of America one cannot fail to like sex. It's not normal. It's not nice."

This paragraph opened a brief essay I wrote a couple of years ago entitled "On Not Liking Sex." The essay, which I have preserved here in quotation marks, was a brittle, glittery piece, a kind of spun confection of the verbal play I'd like to engage in at cocktail parties but can muster only at a solitary desk with a legal-size yellow pad in front of me. It was, in fact, as you can see if you read it straight through, cocktail party chatter. And yet it was true, insofar as any truth can be translated into words. That is, it said some things, and suggested others, about me and the times I live in which were accurate enough as far as they went. 79

But they certainly didn't go very far. Hardly to the end of the block. Certainly not across the street. This essay is an almost perfect example of a phenomenon I've only recently become aware of, though clearly at a deeper level I've understood its workings for a very long time, a kind of pretense at serious writing which I use to keep busy and out of trouble: the kind of trouble you get when you run smack into an idea so significant and powerful that the impact jars you to the bone. It's a way of staying out of the traffic. It is not babble, and it is not easy. On the contrary, it requires painstakingly chosen diction, deliberately controlled syntax, and seamless organization. A rough spot is a trouble spot, a split, a crack, out of which something dreadful (probably black, probably with a grin) may leap and squash you flat.

If this essay was an exercise in making careful statements that would ensure that I never said what I really had to say, then what did I have to say? I don't know. If I'd known then, I couldn't have written such a piece in the first place. And the only progress I've made since then is to have gained a little courage in the face of things that leap out of cracks in the pavement. If I look at the essay again closely, if I listen for the resonances among the words with the not-yet-words, perhaps I can discover some portion of the significance—for the woman just turned forty in the 1980s in the United States of America—of not liking sex.

The title and the first paragraph, by using words as though, like algebraic notation, they had fixed meanings in the context of a given problem, claim to have signified an attitude they have in fact obscured. Even if *on* and *not* may be allowed a certain fixity as they function here, *liking* and *sex* may not. *Sex*, in its most general sense, is simply the way one is: male or female just as black or brown, blue- or hazel-eyed, long- or stubby-fingered, able or not to curl one's tongue into a tube. The genes take care of it. One may dislike one's sex, apparently, just as my daughter dislikes her nose, which is round and tends toward rosy under the sun; some people, thanks to the technological genius of modern medicine, even change theirs. But I like my sex. I suffer from penis envy, of course, to the extent that freedom and privilege have attached themselves to this fleshy sign; I've never wished for the actual appendage, however, except on long car trips through sparsely populated areas. In fact, looked at this way, *not liking sex* doesn't make sense to me at all, any more than do *having sex, wanting sex, demanding sex, refusing sex.* Such phrases clarify the specialized use of the word as shorthand for sexual activity, particularly sexual intercourse.

So I don't like sexual activity. But *like* can mean both to take pleasure in, enjoy, and to wish to have, want; and wanting something seems to me quite a different matter from enjoying it. The former is volitional, a reaching out for experience, whereas the latter is a response to an experience (whether sought for or not) already in progress. In these terms I can and often do enjoy sex. But I do not necessarily want to engage in sexual activity even though I may enjoy doing so.

"The human psyche being the squirmy creature that it is, I have trouble pinning down my objections to sex. I do not seem to object to the act itself which, if I can bring myself to commit it, I like very well. I object to the idea. My objections are undoubtedly, in part, Puritanical. Not for nothing did John Howland, Stephen Hopkins, Thomas Rogers, and Elder William Brewster bring on the Mayflower the seed that would one day bloom in me. If it feels good, it's bad. Sex feels good. My objections may also be aesthetic: It's a sweaty, slimy business. Certainly they are mythic, Eros and Thanatos colliding in the orgasm to explode the frail self back into the atoms of the universe. Love is Death."

The human psyche squirms indeed, especially when it is striving to distance itself from its desires by creating platonic distinctions between things in themselves and the ideas of things. I don't object to the idea of sex. In fact, I don't feel any particular response one way or the other to the idea of sex. Sex for me as for most, I should think, is not ideational but sensual, and it is this distinction that gives me trouble, a distinction that resembles that between wanting and enjoying. I don't object to the *idea* of sex: I object to the *sense* of sex. An act is a sign. Directly apprehended, it has always at least one meaning and usually a multiplicity of meanings. These I must sort out—their implications, their resonances—in order to understand how I, with a singularly human perversity, can not want what I enjoy.

Puritanism, aesthetics, and myth all play a part in this response, no doubt, though the reference to the Mayflower is misleading (the Pilgrims were not Puritans, though many of their descendants were), and as far as I know, the Puritans did not prohibit the sex act—no matter what it felt like—so long as it was confined to the marriage bed. The kind of puritanism that has dogged me is more diffuse than that of my foremothers, perhaps the inevitable legacy of their hard-scrabble existence in tiny communities clinging to the flinty, bitter-wintered New England coast, no longer a religion but still a code of conduct, close-mouthed, grudging of joy, quick to judge and reject. We conducted ourselves at all levels with restraint. Our disapproval of Catholics was not particularly theological; rather, we thought them primitive, childishly taken with display, with their candles and crosses and croziers, play-acting at religion. We painted our houses white with black or green shutters, grey with blue shutters, sometimes soft yellow or dark brown, and we shuddered at the pink and turquoise and lime green on the little capes and ranches that belonged, we assumed, to the Italians. When we met, we greeted one another with a nod, perhaps a small smile, a few words, a firm handshake, even a kiss on the cheek, depending on the degree of our intimacy, but we did not fall into each other's arms with loud smackings, everybody jabbering at once. As a child I was given to fits of weeping and outbursts of delight which to this day my mother refers to with a sigh as "Nancy's dramatics"; I do not, of course, have them now.

Here is the real aesthetics of the matter: the refinement of decoration and gesture to a state so etiolated that voices pierce, perfumes smother, colors clash and scream and shout. I still dislike wearing red and certain shades of pink and orange. The entire sensory world impinges— presses, pinches, pummels—unless one keeps a distance. Touch comes, eventually, to burn. Sex isn't bad so much because it feels good as because it's poor form—the kind of rowdy, riotous behavior one squelches in children as they become young ladies (honest to God, I was never permitted to refer to female human beings as women but only as ladies) and gentlemen. Sex is indecorous.

As for the sweat and slime, the basis for this objection strikes me as more medical than aesthetic. After all, one can get a good deal grubbier on a hike up a small mountain, which is just good clean fun. But the body itself is not clean. It is, according to pathologists like my ancestor Rudolf Virchow, a veritable pesthouse. I grew up knowing that my breath was pestilent ("cover your mouth when you sneeze"), that my mouth was pestilent ("don't kiss me—you've got a cold"). And then along came men, themselves crawling with germs, who breathed on me, who wanted to put their mouths on mine and make me sick. Rudolf may have done wonders for German public health, but he sure put a kink in my private sex life. Oddly enough, this phobia of germs did not include my genitalia, perhaps because they lay untouched and unpondered until long after it had been formed. Nowadays, with the threat of venereal disease widely publicized, I don't suppose one can be so insouciant. The germs lurk at every orifice, and sex is simply contrary to good sanitary practices.

Poor sanitary practices may give you a cold or a stomach flu or herpes, but they are not, in Tucson in 1983, likely to do you in. The equation of sex with death is of another order altogether, though not the less dreadful for not being literal. As late as the Renaissance *to die* was used as we use *to come* to signify orgasm; and although we have abandoned the explicit connection, we have not lost the construct that underlies it. Orgasm shares, briefly, the characteristics we imagine death to have, the annihilation (or at least the transmogrification) of consciousness, the extinction of the *I* that forms and controls being. The loss of my hard-won identity, even for an instant, risks forfeiture of self: not perhaps the death that ends in the coffin but certainly the death that ends in the cell: I am afraid of going away and never coming back.

"But most strongly, my objections are what I reluctantly term 'political.' My reluctance stems from the sense that 'political' in this context implies the kind of radical lesbianism that suggests that medical technology is sufficiently advanced to permit the elimination of the male entirely. I learned, in one of the most poignant affairs of my life, that I am not lesbian. Nor am I even a good feminist, since I seldom think abstractly and tend to run principles together like the paints on a sloppy artist's palette, the results being colorful but hardly coherent. No, when I say 'political,' I mean something purely personal governing the nature of the relationship between me and a given man. In this sense, sex is a political act. In it, I lose power, through submission or, in one instance, through force. In either case, my integrity is violated; I become possessed."

Here's the heart of the matter—politics—and I've dashed it off and done it up with ribbons of lesbianism and feminism so that the plain package hardly shows. True, I'm not lesbian, but thanks to the fundamental heterosexual bias of our culture no one would be likely to assume that I was. And I am, in fact, a perfectly good if unsystematic feminist. Who in my audience, I wonder, was I worried about when I made that self-deprecatory moue, as if to say, "Don't expect too much of me; I'm just a nonradical heterosexual little woman, a bit daffy perhaps, but harmless"? And what the hell (now that I've got the ribbons off) is in the box that made me wrap it up so tight?

83

Politics. Power. Submission. Force. Violation. Possession. Sex is not merely a political act; it is an act of war. And no act is ever "purely personal." It is a nexus that accretes out of earlier and other acts older than memory, older than dreams: the exchange of women, along with goods, gestures, and words, in the creation of allies; the ascription to women of all that lurks terrible in the darkened brain; the protection and penetration of the maidenhead in rituals for ensuring paternity and perpetuating lineage; the conscription of women's sons for the destruction of human beings, of women's daughters for their reproduction; enforcement of silence; theft of subjectivity; immurement; death. If I think that what I do, in or out of bed, originates in me, I am a much madder woman that I believe myself to be. I am no original but simply a locus of language in a space and time that permits one—in politics as in sex—to fuck or get fucked. Aggression is the germ in all the words.

From such an angle, sex is always rape, and indeed I tangle the two words at the level just below articulation. Perhaps I do so because my first sexual intercourse was a rape. At least it occurred in the safety of my own bed by someone I knew intimately, so that although I was furious, I was never in fear for my life. We were both nineteen, had been high-school sweethearts grown apart, and he had come to spend a weekend at the Farm, where I was working as a mother's helper for the summer. We spent the evening deep in conversation, I remember, and after I went to bed, he came into my room, jumped on top of me, deflowered me, and went away again. I don't believe we ever exchanged a word or an embrace. I felt some pain, and in the morning I found blood on my thighs and on the sheets, which I had secretly to wash, so I know that all of this really happened, but I never permitted myself the least feeling about it, not as much as I might have given a nightmare. I *knew* that I was furious, but I *felt* nothing. I don't know what response he expected, but he got none at all. He left the next day, without my ever having spoken to him, and we never met again.

Nor do I know what effect he intended his act to have. I'm sure that he was marking me, for we grew up at the tail end of the time when virginity had real significance, and in defloration he claimed me in only a slightly more subtle manner than incising his initials into some hidden area of my flesh. He knew that I was in love with another man, that I planned to be married within a year, and for a long time I believed that he was trying, through some sort of magical thinking, to force me to marry him instead. We really did believe that a woman belonged to the man who first "had" her. But now I think that he wasn't marking me for himself so much as spoiling me for George. Whatever its true interpretation, his act makes clear my absence from the transaction.

The business was between him and George, the item of exchange one tarnished coin.

To sense myself such a cipher robs me of power. In sex, as in many other instances, I feel powerless. Part of this feeling arises from the fact that, as new symptoms of multiple sclerosis appear and worsen, my power literally drains away. But to what extent is multiple sclerosis merely the physical inscription of my way of being in the world? In sex, as in the rest of my life, I am acted upon. I am the object, not the agent. I live in the passive voice. The phallus penetrates me; I do not surround, engulf, incorporate the phallus. No wonder Caleb raped me. Rape was his only grammatical option.

Thus, I see that in a queer and cruel way I raped him by forcing him to rape me. I always made myself the object of his desire. How many times, I remember now, we came to the brink of intercourse, and always at the last I turned him away, pretending that I couldn't overcome my moral scruples. What I really couldn't overcome was a barrier so ludicrous that I don't expect you to believe it: my underpants. I couldn't figure out how to get rid of them. The women in films and romantic novels, where I'd gotten my impressions of the mechanics of intercourse, didn't struggle with underpants. Did I think they just melted away? After all, I took my underpants off every day as matter-of-factly as I kicked them under the bed to drive my mother wild with despair over my inability to keep some man a decent house. Why then could I not just take them off an extra time? The gesture seemed too overt, too clumsy and pedestrian for the occasion. I couldn't bear to look a fool. So I lay in bondage to the concept of woman as image, not agent, kept a virgin till I was nineteen by Carter Lollipop Pants, red ones and navy ones, their combed cotton grim as iron through my crotch. But for Caleb, who knew nothing of my quandary, I was withholding a treasure that must have seemed of great worth, since I guarded it so jealously. I think I can understand his fury when I threatened to give it to someone else.

Ah, but I'm so old now. I can't blame myself for having been a fool, or him for having believed me a pearl of great price instead of a human being, for whatever she was worth. We were both too young to give tongue to the grammar of our intercourse. All I can do now is use the leverage of my understanding to pry open the box I have stripped and look at the contents squarely. In sex, that political act, I lose power because I have still not learned what it might be and how to claim it.

"For this reason, I have preferred casual lovers to a permanent, long-term partner. They have fewer expectations, thus minimizing possession and obligation. Less is at stake. With them, I can concentrate on the act itself without worrying about its implications. They will be gone long before they learn enough about me to threaten my privacy or come to consider sexual access a right or even a privilege. But even lovers, the romantic ones at least, are risky. They can be more interested in being in love than in bed. My latest lover pitched me out on the grounds that he wasn't in love with me (don't ask me why he took me in—life is complicated enough as it is); and with the irony that won't work in fiction but does splendidly in life, I had fallen in love with him, only the second time that I have done so and the only time that doing so was a mistake. The experience was so nearly disastrous that I learned precipitously the lesson that had long been floating just outside the periphery of my vision: Celibacy is power."

An agoraphobe, a depressive, I have long since learned that avoidance is the most comfortable way to cope with situations that make me uneasy, and God knows sex makes me uneasy. In the playfulness of the opening of a sexual relationship, the issue of power is eclipsed by curiosity, exhilaration, voluptuousness. I find my delight in the process chronicled in my journal: "I sit beside Richard. It is terribly hot—I can feel the steam from both our bodies. We play the touching game—arms touch, knees brush, shoulders press together—at first by 'accident,' testing for response, then deliberately. I love this game, as often as I've played it and as silly as it is; it has a kind of rhythm and elegance when played properly, with good humor, without haste. Richard is very good at it. When, at one point, we have looked at one another for a long moment, he smiles a little and I say, 'What?' He starts to say something, then breaks off: 'You know.' I laugh and say, 'I've been wondering what would happen if I leaned over and kissed you.' It is a dumb idea—I don't know most of the people there very well, but Richard does, and they all know that I'm married. 'I think we'd better wait to do that on our own,' he replies. 'Soon.' 'Yes,' I say, 'yes, soon.' If I hadn't driven my own car, it could have been right then. Wasn't. The kiss is yet to come."

86 But in truth I do not like sex, even in brief affairs. In the rush of excitement I think I do, but afterwards I am always embarrassed by it. If I could stay balanced in the delicious vertigo of flirtation, I might not

feel ashamed, but I can't. I always want to tumble dizzily into bed. And after I've been there, even once, my privacy has been not merely threatened but ruptured. My privacy I carry around me as a bubble of space. Quite literally. I hate to be touched. I hate to be known. If the bubble is pricked, I may disintegrate, leaking out vaporously and vanishing on the wind. The man who has even once seen me up close, naked and transported, knows more about me than I can bear for him to know. For this reason, I have not, in fact, preferred casual lovers to a permanent, long-term partner; if I had, I wouldn't still be married after twenty years. I have taken a casual lover every now and then in the hope that I can reduce sex to pure, unfreighted fun; but the baggage always catches up with me.

One of the cases, of course, carries love. Lovers and husbands alike are risky to a woman who cannot bear to be loved any more than to be touched. I can feel love creep around me, pat me with soft fingers, and I stiffen and struggle for breath. By contrast, I quite readily fall in love and have loved, in some way, all but one of the men I've slept with. So what all the bobbing and weaving about my "latest lover" might mean I'm not sure. I hadn't, at the time I wrote the essay, got over him, and my immediate judgment now is that one oughtn't to try to write the truth while in the kind of turmoil that at that time was threatening my sanity and therefore my life. But on second thought I see that here are simply two truths. I wrote the truth when I said that I'd fallen in love with only two lovers in my life, though I can't think now who I had in mind; I write the truth when I say that I've fallen in love with all but one. Quod scripsi, scripsi. Anyway, I must have learned some lesson from the bitterness the last one brought me, for I have not taken another.

All the same, celibacy is not power. Celibacy is celibacy: the withholding of oneself from sexual union. When it is actively chosen as a means of redirecting one's attention, as it is by some religious, it may both reflect and confer personal power. But when it is clutched at as a means of disengaging oneself from the tentacles of human conflict, it is simply one more technique for avoiding distress. As I stay at home to avoid agoraphobic attacks, I stay out of bed to avoid claustrophobic ones. I am celibate not for the love of God but for the fear of love.

"Avoiding sex altogether is not difficult. You must simply rent a tiny apartment, large enough only for yourself and possibly a very small black cat, and let no one into it. If you want friends, meet them at their houses, if they'll have you, at bars and restaurants, at art galleries, poetry readings, concerts. But don't take them home with you. Keep your space inviolate. During attacks of loneliness and desire, smoke cigarettes. Drink Amaretto. Throw the I Ching. Write essays. Letting someone into your space is tantamount to letting him between your legs, and more dangerous, since you risk his touching the inner workings of your life, not merely your body. Ask him if he wouldn't rather drive into the country for a picnic."

This advice is sound. I have tested all of it. Then I swallowed a handful of Elavil one Hallowe'en and almost succeeded in avoiding sex altogether.

"All this I have learned. What I haven't learned is what to do with the grief and guilt that not liking sex inevitably arouses. The grief is so protean and private that I will not attempt to articulate it. But the guilt is a decidedly public matter, since it could not exist—not in its present form anyway—in the absence of post-Freudian social pressure to regard sex as the primary source not of joy (I doubt that contemporary society knows much about joy) but of satisfaction. If I don't like sex, I am abnormal, repressed, pathetic, sick—the labels vary but the significance is consistent—I do not belong in the ranks of healthy human beings, health requiring as one of its terms sexual activity and fulfillment."

By separating out grief from the complex of responses I feel to not wanting sex, and by tying it off as a "private" matter, I hoped perhaps that, like a vestigial finger or toe, it would drop away. But the dissociation is not authentic, because in fact all my responses are private insofar as the construct they form is my peculiar *I*, and all are public insofar as that *I* is a linguistic product spoken by a patriarchal culture that insists that my God-created function is to rejoice, through my person, the heart of a man. Moreover, failure to do so results not in guilt, as I have stated it, but in shame, which is a truly protean (and, say some feminists, distinctively feminine) emotion, pervasive and inexpiable. About guilt one can do something: Like a wound in the flesh, with proper cleansing it will heal, the scar, however twisted and lumpy, proof against infection. Shame, like the vaginal wound always open to invasion, is an inoperable state. My tongue has given me these distinctions. With it I must acknowledge my shame.

Shamelessness, like shame, is not a masculine condition. That is, there is no *shameless man* as there is a *shameless woman* or, as my grandmother used to say, a *shameless hussy.* A man without shame is in general assumed simply to have done nothing he need feel guilty about. A woman without shame is a strumpet, a trollop, a whore, a witch. The connotations have been, immemorially, sexual. Here is the thirteenth-century author of the *Ancrene Riwle,* a priest instructing three anchoresses in the correct manner of confession: "A woman will say, 'I have been foolish' or 'I had a lover,' whereas she should confess, 'I am a stud mare, a stinking whore.'" And somewhat later, in the *Malleus Maleficarum,* a warning to Inquisitors: "All witchcraft comes from carnal Lust which is in Women insatiable." My sexuality has been the single most powerful disruptive force mankind has ever perceived, and its repression has been the work of centuries.

Now, suddenly, the message has changed. Now, after ages of covering my face and my genitals—St. Paul's veil over my hair, my breasts bound, my waist girded in whalebone, my face masked with kohl and rouge, my length swathed in white cambric pierced by a lace-edged buttonhole through which to guide the erect penis to my hidden treasure—I am supposed to strip to the skin and spread my legs and strive for multiple orgasm.

Knowing what The Fathers have given me to know of the dangers of female sexuality, how could I dare?

"If I got this message from one person at a time, I might be able to deal with it with rationality, distance, even amusement. But I get it impersonally, from all sides, in a barrage so relentless that the wonder is that I survive my guilt, let alone cope with it. I get the message from the bookshelves, where I find not only *The Joy of Sex* but also *More Joy of Sex,* written by a man whose very name promises physical contentment. (I have read some of these books. They contain many instructions on how to do it well. I know how to do it well. I just don't know whether I want to do it at all.) The message comes with my jeans, which I may buy no longer merely for durability and comfort but for the ache they will create in some man's crotch. It foams in my toothpaste, my bath soap. even my dish detergent. It follows me through the aisles of the supermarket and the drugstore. It ridicules my breastless body, my greying hair."

Or has the message really changed? The body swaddled has become the body naked but it is, all the same, the female body, artifice of desire, still inscribed after stripping with the marks of straps cut into the shoulders, underwires into the breasts, zipper into the belly, squeezed and shaved and deodorized until it is shapely and sanitary enough to arouse no dread of its subjective possibilities. The mechanics of its eroticism have been altered so that, instead of receiving male desire as a patient vessel, it is supposed to validate male performance by resonating when it is played upon. Nonetheless, it remains a thing, alien, "other," as Simone de Beauvoir has pointed out, to the man who dreams of it—and also to the woman who wears it, sculpturing it to the specifications of the male-dominated advertising, publishing, fashion, and cosmetic industries.

An object does not know its own value. Even a sentient being, made into an object, will feel uncertain of her worth except as it is measured by the standards of the agora, the market place, which will reflect whatever male fantasies about women are current. Thanks to astonishing technological advances in the broadcasting of these standards, almost everyone in the world knows what they are and can weigh his object or her self against them, no matter how bizarre the means for their attainment may be. Somewhere I read that it takes the concerted pushing and pulling of three people to get a high-fashion model zipped into her jeans and propped into position for photographing. We all see the photographs, though not the three laborers behind them, and believe that the ideal woman looks like that. Thus a standard has been fixed, and most of us, lacking the appropriate sturdy personnel, won't meet it.

Through such manipulation I have learned to despise my body. I have, perhaps, more reason than most for doing so, since my body is not merely aging but also crippled. On the fair market, its value is slipping daily as the musculature twists and atrophies, the digestive system grinds spasmodically, the vision blurs, the gait lurches and stumbles. But long before I knew I had multiple sclerosis, I hadn't much use for it. Nor have I had much use for the man who desires it. He lacks taste, it seems to me: the kind of man who prefers formica to teak,

90

Melmac to Limoges, canned clam chowder to bouillabaisse. Who wants to have sex with a man who can't do better than you?

"Were I living in the Middle Ages, my difficulty could be quickly solved. I would become an anchoress, calling from my cell, 'And all shall be well, and all manner of thing shall be well.' God would love me. My fellow creatures would venerate me. But the wheel has turned and tipped me into a time when God has been dead for a century and my fellow creatures are likely to find me more pitiable than venerable. I shall no doubt be lonelier than any anchoress.

Nonetheless, my bed will stay narrow."

I love closure. Especially in any kind of writing. I like to tie off the tale with some statement that sounds as though nothing further can be said. Never mind the Princess's hysterical weeping on the morning after her wedding night, her later infidelities, the first son's cleft palate, the Prince's untimely death during an ill-advised raid on a neighboring kingdom, the old King's driveling madness: They lived happily ever after, or, if the tale is a modern one like mine, unhappily ever after. But their development ceased. I love closure enough to pretend that quick resolution lies along the length of a cell (in which I might prostrate myself praying not "All shall be well" but "I am a stud mare, a stinking whore"), enough to believe that virtue lies easy in a narrow bed. True, at the time I wrote the essay I was sleeping alone in a narrow bed, but it's widened again now to queen size, with George in one half, or sometimes two thirds, and often Vanessa Bell and Lionel Tigress too.

My sexuality is too complicated a text to be truncated neatly at any point. What has woven it together until now, I see, to prevent it from being a mere tangle of random terror and revulsion, has been my coherent inverse equation of autonomy with physical violation. Such a connection is predicated upon the denial of my own subjectivity in sexual experience. Afraid of being reduced by another to an object, I have persisted in seeing myself as such. Why did I lie, limp as a doll, while Caleb butted at me? Why didn't I writhe, scratch, bite? Why didn't I at least give him a thorough tongue-lashing the next morning before he left my life forever? Over and over I have demanded that I be raped and have then despised both the rapist and myself.

I understand now some of the teachings that helped me compose such a tale of invasion, illness, self-immolation. And I will not close it

91

off with an *ever after,* happy or unhappy. Tomorrow the Princess gets out of bed again: She washes her hair, drinks her coffee, scribbles some pages, tells a joke to her son, bakes a spinach quiche. And the day after. And the day after that. All the while she is telling herself a story. In it, she is aging now, and she drags one foot behind her when she walks. These are changes she can scrutinize in her mirror. They tell her that the true texts are the ones that do not end but revolve and reflect and spin out new constellations of meaning day after day, page after page, joke after joke, quiche after quiche. She has been learning much about vision and revision. She has been learning much about forgiveness. In this story, she is the writer of essays. She has a black typewriter and several reams of paper. One day, she thinks, she could find herself writing an essay called "On Liking Sex." There's that to consider.

On Keeping Women In/Out

My friend Richard is living now with his lover, Helen, in the largish New England town where I spent part of my childhood. From time to time he writes me letters about his work (he is a writer) and his body (he has chondomalacia of the patella) and Helen. I have never met Helen, but I gather from Richard that she suffers periodic episodes of depression and anxiety which keep her occasionally hospitalbound and often housebound. The symptoms ring the whole nine tailors for me, as they must for hundreds, thousands of women—I can't even imagine how many, having only recently begun to be aware that they exist at all. An irony of leading a life as involuted as mine is that you can't find out who else is living as you do and thus, deprived of community, your isolation can only intensify. Starting alone, you grow aloner and aloner, if such a movement is possible.

Plainly Richard has been having trouble dealing with Helen's way of being. He seems, in fact, to have an uncanny knack for involving himself with women in difficulty (they are crippled or anorexic, they have been beaten by former lovers, they run in confusion after other men or women, they try to kill themselves), in which he is surpassed only by my friend Don, one of whose lovers dropped into a psychotic abyss right while he was making love to her. To my horror, Richard seems to have struck on a device for consoling himself about Helen's problems. In his latest letter he tells me, "The people here are pretty understanding about Emily Dickinson types, too, so I'm expecting things to work out now." His solution is a common and comprehensible one for a lover of literature: When something in your life makes you fearful, find a literary analogue (and this one was ready to hand, since Helen is a poet). The process doubtless is not peculiar to literati. Baseball players probably take heart from Babe Ruth, astrophysicists from Stephen

Hawking, missionaries from Father Damien. Courage is not intrinsic, I think; we pass it one to another like the baton in a relay race. "Carry on!" we cry. "Carry on!"

Through our models we choose our lives. And out of this belief arises my horror at Richard's otherwise ordinary inclination to come to terms with Helen's behavior because it resembles that of an admirable poet. It is always dangerous to assign a model to someone else, I think, and it is particularly dangerous to do so out of a desire to deny the pain and complexity of a current situation. A model is always, necessarily, reductive: Unable to know another's life whole, we extract details, generally those that best suit us, disregarding the matrix that gives those details their weight and significance, and thereby attempting to disregard the very different matrix that is the life of the person for whom we have chosen the model. Most dangerous of all, I have found, is the choice of a model for a woman, especially when that woman is an artist.

For the doom of centuries has rendered those two words—*woman* and *artist*—antinomic; and those women who have resisted the enforcement of silence that would stifle their creations have done so often at staggering expense. As far back as poor Margery Kempe, struggling to validate her public utterance of mystical visions, and "Mad Madge" Cavendish, trailing around London in her bizarre costumes, the price has often been the kind of public rejection and ridicule that leave a woman shivering, clad only in her gifts, at least at the door of madness, often all the way into the institution. And, as Virginia Woolf well knew when she created the figure of Shakespeare's sister in *A Room of One's Own*, the outcome of that madness has often been suicide. These points are undeniable. But they are not inevitable. When a woman chooses— or has chosen for her—a model whose life has been crippled by the conflicts generated by the possession of a "male" power, creativity, in a culture that forbids her its use, then she is accepting crippledness, even death, as her inevitable due.

I don't know as much as I'd like of Emily Dickinson. I know the bare biographical facts, of course, especially that, dressed only in white, she confined herself for the last twenty years or so of her life to her father's grounds and house, sometimes to one room in that house, seldom receiving visitors, busying herself with household tasks and horticulture when she was not writing some of the most extraordinary poetry ever produced by anyone, man or woman. I have read a fair number, though by no means all, of the nearly two thousand poems she wrote but re-

94

fused to publish, as well as some of her letters, many of which achieve the quality of her poems.

I have also read some unusually fine feminist criticism that attempts to locate the poems within the matrix of her life, as well as the life within the matrix of her poems. Essentially, the critics come to the same conclusion: that, unable to be both *poet* and *woman*—especially woman defined by the puritanical nineteenth-century mores of a small New England town—she had to reject the latter role. Such a rejection could not be forceful, of course, since force is a masculine trait; instead, it was thoroughly ladylike, a genteel withdrawal, holding her forbidden "male" gift close to her white breast, from the demands and expectations of patriarchal culture to a room in which she could exercise that gift in secret, without offense, no matter how explosive and threatening its products. As Adrienne Rich retells the story, she once pretended to lock the door of her room behind herself and her niece, saying, "Mattie: here's freedom." Suzanne Juhasz, noting the "double bind" of the woman poet, whose womanliness demands self-denial while her art demands self-assertion, sees Dickinson's "movement into her house and then her room as paralleling the movement into her mind that her poems document, because both actions were undertaken for the purpose of maintaining her self against pressures from the world to lose it"—the pressures, specifically, of marriage and motherhood. She saved herself from such a fate, but "ironically," Sandra M. Gilbert and Susan Gubar point out in *The Madwoman in the Attic*, "she discovered that the price of her salvation was her agoraphobic imprisonment in her father's household, along with a concomitant exclusion from the passionate drama of adult sexuality." To escape the constraints of womanhood and affirm herself as an artist meant "denying essential aspects of herself and relinquishing experience as lover, wife, and mother," Albert Gelpi says in his discussion of "My life had stood—a Loaded Gun—," and confronting the "essential paradox of art," that the "loss of a certain range of experience might allow her to preserve what remained; that sacrifice might well be her apotheosis, the only salvation she might know," whereby "she is empowered to kill experience and slay herself into art." "Nevertheless," Gelpi concludes, " 'My life had stood—a Loaded Gun—' leaves no doubt that a woman in a patriarchal society achieves that triumph through a blood sacrifice. The poem presents the alternatives unsparingly: be the hunter or the doe"—be the poet or the woman.

But Richard takes pride in his refusal to read literary criticism, which he sneers at as the whimperings of failed artists or the murderous plots of antiartists, and so he is not likely to have in mind this welter of themes and images—double binds and self-immolation, confinement in the father's house, bridal gown/ghost sheet/shroud, freedom, madness, death—when he identifies Helen with Emily Dickinson. More probably, if he thinks of Dickinson in concrete terms at all, he thinks of the pretty New England town, not unlike the one he and Helen are living in now, and the capacious red-brick house, hardly a tomb; of pattering footsteps and posies and white piqué; of the shy little (her dress is "larger than most readers would have expected," comment Gilbert and Gubar) girl ("Dickinson was fifty-five when she died," notes Rich), whose reticence and reluctance to publish endear her to a culture that values feminine modesty and silence. He thinks not of the woman who had to live out every day of those fifty-five years on some terms but of the "romantic recluse," as the blurb on my copy of her letters calls her, quaint, quirky, but lovable.

Perhaps I should forgive Richard this vision. He is, after all, an earnest young man with a strong will to be kindly, who has never deliberately driven his women to psychic fragmentation and suicide. And his own romanticism predisposes him to romantic interpretation. He likes to think of himself as emotionally "ruined," deadened, incapable of extremes of joy and pain, and for this reason he admires the ability of others to scale heights, plumb depths. He believes in the merit of suffering, and in the particular merit of the artist's suffering. In such a rationale, Dickinson's immurement was simply the necessary price for a body of astonishing poetry. Perhaps so. It's easy to think so now, a century later, with the poems a *fait accompli* and the life that produced them long since stilled. It's easy, too, to make the leap from that life to other lives: If it was good enough for Emily, it's good enough for Helen. That's just the way things are. Out of excruciation springs art.

No. I will not forgive Richard this vision.

From this distance, there's not much I can do about Helen; she'll have to take care of herself. Over the years, as I've slowly come to consciousness, I've developed some sense of sisterhood, out of which I can empathize with Helen's swinging moods, her fears. But I've also learned that the violence of my introversion is such that I do not perceive a threat unless it is aimed directly, immediately, at me. Thus, my horror at Richard's easy association of Helen's agoraphobia and self-confinement with Emily Dickinson's is not for Helen, I know. It is for me, like Helen a woman and a poet, in whom the urge to move inward into the house and downward into the grave is so strong, and the struggle against it so terrible, that the tension has come to determine the texture of my life.

I don't remember becoming a writer. I play with the question of origin sometimes—the way lovers play "when did you first know?"—but I can never come up with an answer. The habit of writing runs in the family, and my aunt, the poet Jean Pedrick, likes to claim that she is the dominant gene who determined my fate. Maybe she's right. Maybe at some little kink in my double helix at the moment of conception I became pen-wielder, wordsmith, as I became blue-eyed, female, flat-chested, with a long second toe and also, according to some theories, a propensity for contracting multiple sclerosis. Or, if I prefer nurture to nature, maybe some word of admiration for my first poem ("The wind is a curious fellow," it began) enticed me into this garden of earthly delights, where all the fruits are syllables and sibilance and swirls of black against the white page. Whichever way, I was apparently a writer by the time I was eight, when I wrote and starred—me, the Blessed Virgin—in the fourth-grade Christmas play, and later that year rewrote the story of the Trojan War.

Nor do I remember becoming a depressive. The kind of depression I have is considered unlikely to be of genetic origin, but it is thought to have physiological roots—some chemical imbalance in my brain, perhaps, that leaves me lying awake for hours in the night and takes away my hunger for anything but death. This depression, far more common in women than in men, seems often to be triggered by a disruption in relationships, in which women are schooled to invest far more of their identity and psychic energy than men. I used to associate my depression with the period that I was hospitalized for its treatment in my twenties, but now I understand that it is far older than that. The diaries I kept as a teenager express despair as regularly as they discuss algebra tests, migraines, and Pilgrim Fellowship: "I don't want anything. I can't feel anything. I hate everything. I want to die." By this late point (my senior year in high school), the habit of wishing for death was as ingrained as the habit of writing. I do not, in fact, remember a time that I wasn't overwhelmed by a yearning for wholeness, completion (generally through an ecstatic union with a man), which I knew could not be fulfilled; rather than live without it, I prayed to die. I think now that the death of my father when I was four lies at the root of that unfulfilled longing, but such knowledge comes too late to break the pattern of passion and death that shapes my life.

I do, however, remember becoming an agoraphobe. That is, I dimly remember my first attack, which occurred when I was twenty-three in an Italian restaurant in Boston's North End, where George and I had gone with a large group after an art show or a poetry reading or perhaps a Christmas concert. In the warm red room I felt suddenly as though I couldn't breathe; I was chilled to the bone yet clammy with sweat; I couldn't swallow; I thought I would throw up. This last sensation was the worst, since I have a horror of vomiting. I'd experienced such symptoms before, I think, but that night they came together in a nexus of panic so engulfing, so crippling, that my life congealed around the fear that they would recur. And they did. Unpredictably. Then predictably. I could no longer go to restaurants or theatres. If anyone but George were around, I could not eat. I could not stay in the supermarket long enough to buy a week's worth of groceries. I quit my job. I stopped leaving my apartment building, then my apartment. Finally I stayed crouched in one corner of my livingroom couch, my thoughts reverberating inside my skull as though it were an iron bell, their ringing so loud that, terrified, I would call George at work and beg him to come home. Clearly he couldn't keep coming home—somebody had to support us—and so, on the advice of my psychotherapist, I signed myself into Metropolitan State Hospital and became a certified madwoman.

Something is common in these elements—womanness, poetry, depression, agoraphobia—but the connection lies deep, deeper perhaps than I dare to dive. Since I first began to think about writing this essay I have had trouble breathing, and I write gasping and fainting as though about to go down for the last time. (I think of Emily's breathless little phrases, her dashes and queer capitals and exclamation points, the quick gulps of air between the hard ringing awful words.) Even if I find the connection, bring it up, it will be, you know, some gordian knot, black and slippery with sea muck, and I, swordless, wordless, will be stuck holding it with the tips of my fingers and watching it drip on the rug. It won't be something you or I will understand.

98   Being a writer made me strange. Or I was strange because I was a writer. Since I don't remember either not being a writer or not being strange, I can't tell which of these statements is true. But I do know that

I led what seemed to be an odd existence from the time I was very young, an existence split, not quite cleanly, between an exterior life of almost pure convention and an interior life of almost pure imagination. The two could not, I learned, simply co-exist, and I associate this lesson with an incident that occurred when I was seven. I had a new dress, what today would be called a peasant dress, with a white top and a turquoise skirt, elasticized at the waist and neck. I could pull the top down off the shoulders, a style I thought wonderfully romantic, though I don't know just where I got the idea, since I had seen few movies and no television and I hadn't yet read *Gone with the Wind*. Keeping the off-the-shoulder effect took a good bit of attention, I discovered, since at the slightest exertion the elastic popped back up around my collarbone. But I kept at it, knowing that my loveliness was worth the work, until, on the playground at recess, I heard one of the teachers laugh to another, "That dress certainly keeps Nancy busy, doesn't it?" I felt the blow in my solar plexus. I was, to the world out there, where I could not live but had to move, not lovely but ridiculous. The script I was writing as high drama appeared to others a farce.

Not for thirty years, however, would I understand about inscription: How, whether I was writing or not (I scribbled madly through high school and most of college; got married and stopped dead for eight years; started again for a few years; stopped for a few more; am hard at it again), I was making a life that contained all the standard pieces of a woman's existence—romance and heartbreak, marriage and motherhood, infidelity and shame—I could lay hand to. Nor did I understand the palimpsestic and eclectic nature of the process: How no one makes up her life out of whole cloth, but rather patches together a crazy quilt out of snippets, old and new, tossed at her out of the scripts of others. I took all of them—the folk wisdom, my mother's and grandmother's cautionary tales, the shapely lives of the heroines of historical novels, "Can This Marriage Be Saved?" in the *Ladies Home Journal*, the misguided encouragement/discouragement of teachers and friends—and stitched them into a life so frayed by contradictions that it threatens to come apart at the seams at every moment. Most of these contradictions revolve around the roles of silence and suffering in a script whose central character tries to be simultaneously a woman and an artist.

A woman must not speak. No one ever told me that. "Children"—boys and girls—"should be seen and not heard" was a family maxim, but it was enforced playfully, and then usually to quell bumptious behavior, not conversation. I was often permitted, indeed encouraged, to speak at home, in the classroom, even, on Youth Sunday, from the pulpit.

How, then, did I learn the rule of silence? I think immediately of "The Little Mermaid," one of my favorite fairy tales as a child. In it, you remember, the little mermaid, who has no name, gives her tongue to a sea witch in return for transformation into a human woman, in which form she hopes to gain an immortal soul by winning the love of the Prince. I read the tale over and over, admiring the mute, tearless suffering of the little mermaid, who had sacrificed all for love (I wasn't much taken by immortality), her every step agonizing enough to draw blood, unable to utter either her pain or her adoration. Now I think it a cruel story. Why should the little mermaid have to hang all her hopes for an immortal soul (I care more for such things of late) on the whim of a handsome but certainly thick-headed man? Why should she give up her art—for she loses the power not just of speech but of song, and "she had the loveliest voice of all in the sea or on the earth"—on the off chance that, by looking at him "mildly, but very mournfully," she can win his heart? If she'd kept her tongue, she might have been able to woo him, or—better yet—she might have told him after a while that he was a vain and silly Prince and she'd really rather go off and sing in a cabaret. This I think now. But there was a time when I would have cut my tongue out just to have a chance at the love of a man, and when I believed that I would have to do so to get it.

I think I knew, though, that the rule of silence wasn't absolute. After all, the women in my family, all of whom have had the love of at least one man, gabble without cease and without trepidation. I grew up a gabbler. I learned that the interdiction was not against all women's speech but against certain kinds of utterance. There was women's talk—desultory, incremental, its frequent themes the babies and the neighbors, food, ornament, a weaving of memories, warnings, plans— which stopped abruptly when a man entered the kitchen, crossed the back yard by the wading pool. There was men's talk—earnest arguments about the best left-fielder, the best car, the best man for the job—which didn't cease when a woman came in, though the tone may have shifted somewhat, so long as she sat smiling vaguely and asked no questions. The talk when men and women got together, which formed a middle semantic domain, was a sort of hectic badinage that thrilled and exhausted me, empty of content though not of suggestion, silly I think now, but infinitely promising then. How else could they talk to each other? The women were ashamed to disturb their men with the rash on baby's upper thighs or the dangers of botulism in home-canned beans; the men knew full well that a woman would keep driving a car with the oil light on till the engine froze right up. What had they in common but sex?

In terms of writing, these domains of speech defined my possibilities. I couldn't imagine writing a "woman's" book. What would it be, except maybe a cookbook? How could you write anything interesting that didn't focus on a man? on a woman's passion for a man? Impossible. And I couldn't write a "man's" book—nasty, arid things those were, full of ideas, not feelings, and I hadn't an idea in my head. Or at least if I got one I plucked it straight out, the way we pulled the fat pale-green worms off the tomato plants, before it could chomp its way through my brain. Men didn't have much use for women with ideas. (When I was eleven, I told a grandfatherly man that I planned to be an astronomer, and he hooted with delight. I was just the cutest thing he had ever seen. He rushed to tell his friends, who all said how funny and darling I was.) And I wanted a man *much* more than I wanted to write a book. If I could have chosen to write Harlequin Romances, those epitomical creations of the middle domain, I'd probably have been all right. But for me this writing business has had nothing to do with choice. I needed to write literature, in the way that some creatures aspire to an immortal soul. And I knew whose domain that was.

I gave up writing altogether and went mad in a homely way. I had got everything I wanted more than to write a book: the man of my dreams, and then a daughter for him, and then a fine job to put him through graduate school. I was twenty-three years old, poised, articulate, well-dressed, cultivated. And then one night in an Italian restaurant I stopped breathing.

Agoraphobia. Nowadays the diagnosis is fairly straightforward, and a number of treatments have been tried, some very successfully. But when I first collapsed, more than fifteen years ago, the term was not available to, or at least not current among, the doctors who treated me. One doctor decided, on the basis of the Rorschach and Thematic Apperceptive Tests I was given, that I was schizophrenic and ought to have insulin shock therapy; and initially I was drugged with the powerful antipsychotics given to violent and delusional patients. Violence and delusion, however, were hardly my problems. I was simply, over-whelmingly sad. I hated my wonderful life, built as it was on the assumption that I was competent to lead it, and I wanted to extinguish it as quickly as possible. These are classic depressive symptoms, and before long the doctors at Met State diagnosed me as suffering from "severe depression with anxiety"—accurate enough, but so global that it revealed almost nothing about the condition's etiology and little more about possible treatment. The doctors prescribed antidepressants with tranquilizers and electroconvulsive therapy, and after twenty-one zaps to my brain I cheered up. I left the hospital to return to my family and work, to have another baby, and eventually to start writing again. No one told me what danger that combination of activities put me in; later I found out for myself.

Years afterward, I first heard the term *agoraphobia* used to describe a specific mental condition wherein a person suffered such engulfing symptoms of anxiety at the thought of leaving her own space that she became totally confined in order to ward them off; and I knew what was wrong with me. I'd known the word, of course, since it's part of an etymological game students often play—agoraphobia: the fear of open spaces; acrophobia: the fear of high places; ailurophobia: the fear of cats; hircophobia: the fear of smelling bad. But the definition, because it is unfaithful to the root (agora: the market place), misled me into thinking of "open space" as a mountain top, the desert, the prairie, the shore. Some agoraphobes are afraid of such swept and empty places, but I am not. My agoraphobia translates directly: fear of the market place. Of public space. Of the spot where citizens assemble to discuss and vote on matters of the city-state. Had I been a Greek woman, I would never have entered the agora. I would not, in fact, have left my house. I would not have been a citizen, except in name. Thanks to my agoraphobia, I am still not a citizen.

And I am not alone. A recent text on the subject says that about one in one hundred sixty people suffer from agoraphobia. That there are so many of us at first surprised me. For years I not only had no label for my disease, but I assumed that I alone experienced it. No one ever spoke of having symptoms like mine. But then, I never mentioned my own symptoms, though I hinted at them to a few intimates, who clearly didn't recognize them. Pierced by shame at my own weakness, I denied them, disguised them, compensated for them until most of my energy was spent on subterfuge. To this day, if I have to refuse or cancel an activity because I am having an agoraphobic attack, I will make up some excuse—my head aches, my car has broken down, I have to grade papers—rather than admit that I am gasping and sweating and shitting in terror of having to live in the world. No wonder I don't hear of others. If they have my dis-ease, they likely share my shame.

That at least two-thirds of us are women surprises me not at all. We are the products, individually and collectively, of a cultural tradition of such antiquity that it was already old when the Greek woman was debarred from the agora. We have had to hide while menstruating, cover our heads and swaddle our bodies, lower our eyes, hold our tongues. Not by accident has the process of giving birth, perhaps the most active of human endeavors, been euphemized by a verb used always in the passive, "to be confined." Ours has been a history of confinement: in the childbed, in the crinoline, in the kitchen, even (if all other safe harbors fail) in the asylum. Perhaps in some dark prehistory all women objected to being shut up; perhaps they had to be forced into their caves or cottages and bound by the ankles until their muscular legs atrophied. Certainly throughout the ages some few have burst out of confinement—witness fourteenth-century Margery Kempe discomfitting all the bishops with her public boisterous weeping on her peregrinations through Europe and the Holy Land. But most have needed no turn of an iron key, no leather thong. We've known where we belong. And if we've tried to trespass over the threshold, our hearts have knocked, our mouths have gone dry and our skins damp, our lungs have shriveled, our bowels have let go. There's nothing like the symptoms of agoraphobia for keeping a woman in her place. Let me tell you. Nothing.

But even confined to the house, a woman can always write, can't she? I mean, as long as someone else is willing to venture out to buy the legal-size yellow pads, the black ink, the typing paper and ribbons. After all, Emily did. Thousands of poems.

Well, no. True, Emily did, though she seems to have had a bad time of it nonetheless. Staying at home may increase the opportunities for writing. But agoraphobia is, like all illnesses, ultimately a metaphor. The agora need not be a town square, an office, a classroom, a department store, a friend's livingroom. It is any area perceived as part of the patriarchal domain. For that reason, writing causes me as much anxiety as any other incursion into masculine activity. The symptoms are somewhat different—breathlessness still, but this time accompanied by distractibility (I read dictionaries a lot) and lassitude—and they are somewhat easier to bear because I don't risk exposing them to others. Still, they result in the same self-disgust; and they just as effectively prevent me from doing a man's work. In fact, I swing around a circle of avoidances: Anxious at the act of writing and depressed by its failure, I burst out into the world, seeking distraction and satisfaction there; intimidated by my inadequacies and depressed because I'm not writing, I flee in panic back to my safe house. I can manage to suffer whatever I do.

An artist must suffer in order to create. I grew up believing that maxim, just as I believed the one my mother told me when I was having my thick hair razor-cut, the tears squirting from my eyes with each tug on a lock: "You have to suffer for beauty." The stereotypical artistic suffering was madness. I was terrified of madness because, from a very early age, I believed that I was mad; the discrepancies between my inner and outer lives were too great to be explained in any other way. So I gave up writing and turned to wholesome pursuits, only to crack up anyway. And madness, I learned then, holds nothing of the grandeur of Kirk Douglas's film portrayal of Vincent Van Gogh. It is scrimy, painful, and, to be honest, boring. I don't think that the artist creates because she is mad. I think she wrings out what she can despite the misery and terror, despite the long blank afternoons she spends huddled in one corner of her livingroom couch, the voices resonating around the curve of her skull, the sudden quiet descent into the will for death. And I think she might wring out more if she didn't bleed her time and energy into these states.

I have to write. If I avoid that mandate, I wind up trying to kill myself. It's as simple as that. But I don't have to be scared out of my wits every time I pick up my pen. I don't have to be mad. It's a role I've learned, a way of responding to the conflicts I experience when I step into the market place of the word, a response that people like Richard have reinforced by assuming tacitly that the woman artist is bound to be neurotic. But it's a role I can't afford. Literally. Emily's father was a lawyer who could support her retreat from the world; I have no patriarch to shelter me. Fewer and fewer women do. We don't want them. I want to be thrown out into the world, my pen and pad flung after me, and to sit in the middle of the agora scribbling until my fingers are bone. I want to survive out there, and maybe even have a good time.

It may be too late. I am nearly forty, and I have had time to transform my madness into the rituals that keep me alive as well as dying. But at least I know now that depression and agoraphobia are metaphors, codes in the cultural text in which I am embedded. Not entities. Not the inevitable fate of the woman who trespasses onto the page. I'm a writer. If I can make the chance, I'm sure as hell going to revise them out of this script.

On Loving Men

I would prefer not to.

The first man I loved left me without even saying goodbye, and the loving of men has brought me endless sorrow and travail ever since.

Six days before Christmas in 1947, nearly five months after my fourth birthday and three months after his twenty-eighth, my father ran off the road at night in his jeep and died, likely of a cerebral hemorrhage caused by striking his head on a refrigeration pipe at work earlier in the day rather than in the crash itself. I woke to what I remember as a rainy morning (though I don't know how it could have been, since we were living on Guam, in the South Pacific, where indeed it rained every day, but only in the afternoon) and a house full of weeping women. My sister Sally, who was two and a half, and I were packed off to play with our friends Judylee and Buz Childers, not itself an unusual event, but I see by my use of "packed off" that I had an uneasy sense of haste and disruption, which were unusual in my placid existence. After lunch Bob Childers drove us home again and helped Mother put us to bed for our naps. Daddy always came home for lunch, and he must often have put me to bed. At any rate, I was puzzled by his absence, for as Mother reached to pull the tent of mosquito netting over me, I asked, "Where's Daddy?" "Daddy's dead, Nancy," she said, and I hit her with all my strength in the stomach.

I suppose that I loved him. What else but love could have created a fury so strong, so icy that, despite that blow to my mother's belly, I did not dare to recognize or utter it for decades after his death? But I must have been too young to monitor and label my inward experiences in that anxious manner that became my habit not long afterward, because I don't remember feeling love for him. He was just there, a pervasive presence, enormous (at five feet six inches, he barely met the physical requirements for appointment to the Naval Academy, and I am now only a half inch shorter than he was) and deep-voiced and good-humored.

Rather, I remember him in images, quick vignettes sliced from a reel of colored film. I hear his voice giving directions the time that, when we were living on Truk, my little dog went mad and a group of men had to track her down and shoot her. I am standing beside the toilet balancing a cardboard box on my head as I watch the arc of his pee spurt from above my head and splash into the bowl: "Look what I can do!" I cry, tilting my chin back and forth to keep the box in place, and he admires my cleverness. He stretches out his palm to show me the wriggling tail of a lizard my cat Muffin has tried to catch. He is fishing me, dazed at the light from the open door behind him, out from under the bed where I have dropped and rolled in my sleep. He is driving Mother and Sally and me under the palm trees along a beach where we meet some natives. Only once is he angry, when Sally and I have got into a neighbor's green paint and he and Mother scrub us vigorously with turpentine, which makes Sally, who has terrible heat rash, wail in pain. Another time he chides me for pouring sand into some kerosene flares at a construction site (the whole of Guam is a vast construction site, and he, a civil engineer in the SeaBees, teaches me the names of all the earth-moving equipment), but he doesn't punish me.

And then he is gone. My memories continue, mostly of places, but the places are peopled: with Mother and Sally, of course; with Garm and Pop, Daddy's parents, from whose house we lived only a few blocks when we returned to New England; with Granna and Grandma, Mother's mother and grandmother, whom we visited often; with teachers, after I started school the next fall, and school friends; with dozens of aunts and uncles and cousins. My life was hardly empty, though I was often lonely in it. It simply held no father, and I spent the next fifteen years of my life struggling to close that gap, through which, it seemed to me, all the potential joys of my life leaked out before I could sample or savor them.

I grew up in a household of women. At first Mother, Sally, and I lived in a large old duplex in Exeter, New Hampshire. Since Garm and Pop lived nearby, Pop did his best to fill in for Daddy, taking us stargazing, I remember, and attending Father's Day activities at school; but he was a tease, rough, a tickler, who sang in a loud deep voice and played pig-pile, and I was afraid of his boisterousness. Sally was not, and so she was his favorite, chortling under his strong fingers as he sang, "I Don't Want Her, You Can Have Her, She's Too Fat for Me," or began a story, "Once upon a time, when pigs spoke rhyme and monkeys chewed tobacco. . . ," her hair in blonde pigtails, her blue eyes crinkled above her round cheeks, while I stood back a little, darker, skinny, slightly stiff with longing and fear. But we never lived with him, not even in the summer when we all moved to The Cottage in North Hampton, because he still owned Jack Smith Chevrolet then and spent most of his time there. When I was nine, after Grandma died, we moved with Granna into a new house in Wenham, Massachusetts, and so saw even less of Pop.

I don't think I felt anything intrinsically wrong with living without a man. That is, after the dizzying dislocation that followed Daddy's death, whirled by plane and train half way around the world, plunged from tropical heat, which was all I could remember, into the depths of a New England January, I soon resumed a calm and regulated existence: summers at The Cottage and winters in school, pancakes for supper every Sunday night, Santa Claus at Christmas, the bunny at Easter, and the fairy with her dime after every lost tooth, new clothes in the fall and the spring. My life became an intricate ritual—in many ways still is—in which actions and events occurred in orderly, predictable cycles; when you've had one disruption as drastic as the death of a father, you'll use any magic to hedge against another. In fact, the only disruptions I recall for the next few years, until my mute and patient stepfather joined our household, had to do with men, and my mother's going off with them. Once she went off not just for an evening but for a whole week, leaving Sally with Granna and Grandma, and me with a cousin I barely knew, and just when she was supposed to come rescue me, she got sick and had to spend several days in the hospital. I vowed bitterly that I would never let a man take me away and make me sick.

All the same, I learned that manlessness was a very bad state indeed, and that anyone consigned to it—especially my mother, so young, so pretty—was greatly to be pitied. Not only Mother but also Granna was without a man, having divorced my grandfather, under painful circumstances, many years before. Grandfather was a womanizer, who years after the divorce shot himself dead in a hotel room while following some young thing to California, and thus a "bad" man, whereas Daddy was a "good" man (who got better, of course, over the years, when he was no longer around to make any mistakes), so Granna's lot, I understood, was not tragic like Mother's, but she too—very ambivalently—wanted to have a man. She solved her ambivalence by falling in love with a man who was already married, and she was a genuinely honorable woman who would never have disrupted a marriage, so she managed both to have a man and not to have a man. Thus, by the time I knew her at least, she wasn't looking. But Mother was, or at least people were always on the lookout for her, and so I spent my childhood in an atmosphere of husband-hunting as relentless as, though more subtle than, Jane Austen portrays in *Pride and Prejudice.*

For this reason, perhaps (or perhaps because of some hormonal imbalance—who the hell understands the reasons for such things?), I began my own manhunt early. I don't seem to have enjoyed that latency period promised by the psychoanalysts, for which reason, I suppose, I never much cared for horses. I had my first "friend-boy," as I called him, as early as first grade, maybe kindergarten. His name was Jimmy Bradley, and he was blond. In second grade a boy named Peter and I used to crawl into the big wooden boxes on the playground and talk—briefly, for the teachers always swooped down and pulled us out to play Capture the Flag or Statues. I didn't go to third grade, but the summer between second and fourth I fell in love with my babysitter's boyfriend, a sixteen-year-old lifeguard, and lay night after night in my hot bed at The Cottage, sticky sheets grinding sand into my sunburn, imagining his kiss: the first time I recall sex twining itself into the feelings I identified as love. This confusion was eventually to cause me all kinds of trouble—but more of that later. I returned to boys about my own age: Johnny until I moved to Wenham; Greg, stocky and shy, with fiery hair; a neighbor named Bruce, who wore his hair long and slicked back like Elvis's before I'd ever heard of Elvis, and another, Kirk, who knew how to muck horses and kill chickens, the area we lived in being still semi-agricultural; Kenny, whose bad breath drove me to suck horrid breath mints so that I'd have an excuse to offer him one. In the ninth grade I turned back to an adult, developing a terrific crush (true word: my adoration nearly squeezed the life out of me) on my science teacher, which aroused my sexual feelings to a pitch so fevered that the edges of my life darkened and curled like scorched paper. I saw Mr. Natale again once after I was grown up, in a hospital where we chatted about his son's broken leg and my daughter's eye operation, only I didn't recognize my beloved until that night, drowsing in the dark, when I sat up suddenly and cried, "Mr. Natale!" much to my husband's startlement; I don't suppose Mr. Natale knew me at all.

None of these loves was requited, of course. Whatever would I have done if they had been? Already, I think, I would have been quick to despise the requiter, as I was long afterward; I always lost respect for my boyfriends once I'd started to get them, à la the old joke about refusing to join any club that would take me as a member, and when I was thirty-one, I was still able to write in a poem,

> The man who doesn't love me
> I love twice
> once for his beauty,
> again for his sound sense.

From a very early age I grew accustomed to worshipping in pain and from afar. As time went on, I was the object of some unrequited loves myself, but always from boys I considered wholly unsuitable suitors: Eddie, who came up about to my belly button; Stanley, who was pale and fat; Daniel, whose sense of humor ran to resonant belches in crowds. If they felt any pain at my coldness, I certainly did not know it. Not for many years would I understand that I could genuinely hurt another person, and even today my understanding remains academic, something I know but do not trust. Eddie and Stanley and Daniel, as far as I was concerned, were merely fools; but I was truly tragic. As a woman, I knew, I was destined to suffer greatly for the love of men.

How did I know such a thing? To be sure, my grandfather had been unfaithful to my grandmother, and so, in his own way, had my father been to my mother, abandoning her to the care of two small children and a grief she could never articulate. But they were self-reliant women who did what they had to do, and they didn't talk about their suffering. Rather, my learning must have been largely literary, garnered from the hundreds of books and handful of movies that provided the ground of my imaginative life.

Oh, but I fed my passions fat and purpurescent on the romance of novel and film. I read without cease, indiscriminately. Mother, herself a reader, never restricted my choice of texts, and in fact I remember her marching into the one-room library at the back of the Wenham Town Hall and commanding fat grey-haired Mrs. Joyner to check out to me books from all the shelves, not just those in the children's section. Mrs.

Joyner's jowls quivered, but every week she checked out stacks of Anya Seton and Lawrence Schoonover and Frank Slaughter and Mary Stewart with neither a word nor a frown. The one exception to Mother's permissiveness—when I brought Frank Yerby's *The Saracen's Blade* home from a book sale, she told me she thought I ought to put it away for a couple of years before reading it—so startled me that I put it away for a couple of years before reading it.

The first romantic novel I remember reading, the summer I turned eight, was a sandy copy of *Flash Gordon in the Caverns of Mongo*, which had probably belonged to my father and which I found at The Cottage, wedged in among The Bobbsey Twins and The Five Little Peppers. How I longed to be Dale Arden, swept melting into the arms of the intrepid Flash and whisked away from her pale hideous captors. Shortly thereafter I read *Wuthering Heights* for the first time. Then *Ramona*. Anya Seton's *Katherine*. *Rebecca*. *Jane Eyre*. Later *Kristin Lavransdätter*. *Gone with the Wind*. And those monuments of adolescent egocentricity *Atlas Shrugged* and *The Fountainhead*. These are the ones that stick in my head, because I read them over and over, with innumerable others in between. Too, although Mother didn't take me to the movies often, and I certainly wouldn't have been allowed to go alone, she did take me to *Ivanhoe* and *King Richard and the Crusades*, both starring Robert Taylor, and from then on my ideal lover was tall and black-bearded and impassive, not unlike my husband today. I recall, in one of those quick clear imagaic flashes that make possible the life of the then now, brushing my teeth the morning after I saw *Ivanhoe*, suddenly so overcome with longing for the handsome knight that I had to drop my toothbrush, clench my jaws, and grip the edge of the sink with both hands to keep myself from slipping to the floor and howling in pain.

From these sources I learned of love. It was shattering. Women of otherwise remarkable grit and composure (and the women I liked to read about were no sissies) capitulated before the passionate demands of men, turned their bodies and their lives over to them. For the winning of men they suffered; in the losing of men they suffered. Of course men were capable of suffering too: witness Heathcliff (although he wasn't entirely respectable, was he?). But they were usually absorbed in other activities, most of which involved fighting of some sort, and thus did not keep their suffering pure and focused. I learned, too, that love was remote. It happened in a remote past. An indeterminate fu-

ture. Another country. To women nothing like me. They were volup-
tuous (alas the small bulges on my chest no bigger than doorbells),
beautiful (woe my large mouth crammed with white and silver teeth),
elegant (*waly* my large hands always dropping and knocking, my
bounding walk, my hand-me-down clothes). Not for many years would
I read *Madame Bovary,* but when I did, I would recognize with amusement and chagrin the exotic nature of Emma's romantic fantasies. Fulfillment of the love I knew about, which shook my frame so that I could
hardly brush my teeth, was otherwhen/otherwhere/otherwise.

Then, in the middle of my pedestrian twentieth-century homely
American thirteen-year-old life, I fell in love with a boy who fell in love
with me. And it was wonderful. So wonderful that my entire relationship to Spring—which was, of course, when it happened—has
been colored by it ever since, the scent of rain on apple blossoms and
lilacs making me weak and weepy, and it's a good thing I've moved to
the desert, where we have quite another Spring, or I'd still be useless
every April. It didn't last very long. After a couple of months James lost
interest in me, and then I understood that he had never been in love
with me at all but had only wanted a girlfriend because all his friends
were getting girlfriends (I found this cynical explanation, for some reason, more adult and plausible than the possibility that he had simply
loved me just for a little while), so I was really rather back where I had
started. But not quite. For a short time I had believed myself loved by
someone I adored (James was darkly handsome and intelligent and
wealthy and his father had been at The Naval Academy with my father), and the form of my existence, that long sequence of unrequited
worshippings, was shattered. Thereafter I would seek requital.

So there I was, just turned fourteen, entering my sophomore year in
high school, having primed myself for love with all the fictions my
culture would yield up to my scrutiny together with a sweet fragment of
experience, jilted, true, but determined to have romance again. And
could I get some man to love me? Not on your life. Or rather, I couldn't
get the right man to love me, the one I could worship in return. I could
find plenty of candidates, of course: Bob and Billy and Jeff and John
and Bud. . . . In fact, I lived an emotional life equivalent to a shopping
trip through Filene's Basement, racing in a crush of eager women from
one table to the next, holding up a cashmere sweater, slipping on a pair
of Neiman-Marcus shoes, breathless and sweaty and increasingly desperate. Only in Filene's Basement you get to choose a piece of merchan-

dise and take it home if you like it; you do not have to get it to like you in return. If you did, I'd have had to settle for battered hats, trousers with one leg shorter than the other, a size eighteen dress with chartreuse and turquoise polka dots. Or go home empty-handed. The wrong men continued to love me, sometimes tenaciously—bumbling Gary and lisping Fred and pudgy Alan—all good, I see now, all gentle, but not a romantic figure among them. Instead of feeling grateful to them for proving me lovable, I despised them as incarnations of my failure to get what I wanted, and I despised myself for being able to get nothing but them.

Pictures of myself taken around this time show a young woman with thick, light-brown hair cut in bangs around a small face, greyish blue eyes, a wide mouth with large white teeth, and an unformed body with very long slender legs. Her expression is always stiff, a little glazed, the look of someone who hopes that when the film is developed she'll see a face much prettier than the one she confronts in the mirror. Beyond this slight revelation, they show nothing of an interior life moiled in the terror of madness. For by then I believed that I was going insane, and that only love could rescue me from insanity. I was truly the princess locked in the tower. "Until I find someone to take James's place, some love to replace that most beautiful love," I wrote on 14 January 1959, "I will be tortured to the point of madness." Raised in the tradition of prayer as petition, I prayed alternately for love and death. I don't think it mattered much which.

What I got was love. This time it lasted a couple of years, not a couple of months, and because I was then a compulsive diarist, I have a complete record, in the purplest of prose on cream-colored green-lined paper stitched into black covers, of this affair. Reading it today is a queer experience, for the woman scribbling those pages was younger than my daughter is now, and she seems very far away, as indeed she is: a quarter of a century and the breadth of a continent. I find it hard to believe that I bear her, if not actually in my flesh (haven't my cells completely replaced themselves several times in all these years?), then in the spirit that animates that flesh. And yet I must, since the events she records appear in me as memories. That intimacy acknowledged, however, I return to reading the diaries as though they were a tale, and with good reason, for that's exactly what they are. I have always had to tell myself the story of myself in order to sense a self at all. I assume that everyone does, though perhaps only those of us most intoxicated with language are driven to leave a record of the process.

Here in these black books, then, I have the story of a young woman named Nancy and a young man named Caleb who met and fell in love not long after the middle of the century in a small town on the North Shore of Massachusetts. It follows particular structural and stylistic principles of which the young author was wholly unaware, but by which she was wholly bound, as she wrote. An early work, it prefigures all the author's later stories on similar themes. Though shorter than some and longer than others, it is clearly emblematic of their content and execution. There is not an original word in it.

If, as I now believe, the young Nancy received this story out of a tradition and wrote it in a grammar both so thoroughly immured in female experience as to be inexplicit and unquestioned, then its anatomy—replicated in one relationship after another—ought to reveal at least some of the systematic difficulties I face in loving men. These lie not, as I once believed, in specific qualities or defects in my psyche but rather in my response to conventions imposed on my storytelling which are essentially alien to my way of experiencing the world. That is, I have told myself stories about my love for men in terms appropriate to a masculine narrator because the techniques of my craft available to me I learned from a patriarchal literature I have read in snatches all the way back to the Old Testament.

Of the conventions taught to me, the most basic is the linearity of narrative structure. A story has a beginning, a middle, and an end. I fell in love with Caleb on Valentine's Day 1959 at a Pilgrim Fellowship dance. This isolatable event is odd except within the story, since we lived in a town of about twenty-five hundred people and, even though he was a grade behind me in school, we must have known each other for years. But there you have it: Valentine's Day. He did not fall in love with me, and with a tenacity remarkable in a woman prone to fantasizing a new love as often as once a week, I pursued him yearningly, mostly on the old yellow bus that shuttled us between our village and a nearby city high school. Finally, five months later almost to the day, he capitulated; and I suppose if he were telling the story, here would be his beginning.

For me it was a kind of end. All the tales I knew told of getting a man, not of having him. There were certain obstacles to be overcome, I knew: the antipathy of families, for instance, or the incarceration of one party or the other. In my case, the obstacle was largely indifference, not very glamorous, but trying enough. Once I had overcome it, however, I simply didn't know what to do next. In the tales the lovers lived "happily ever after," a formula that failed to provide a blueprint for the daily meetings and partings—the sharing of books, the making of jokes, the dancing close, the clumsy lovemaking, the telephoning every few hours—of a pair of high-school students neither of whom, in fact, had much idea what it meant to live happily even in this moment, let alone all the next ones. In this matter we were ideally suited: We were both melancholics.

The actual end did not come for a long while; and again, as in the beginning, it came at different times for each of us, I think. For me it couldn't come until I found someone to take Caleb's place, for I had resolved, though not at all consciously, never again to be without a man. Off and on I made abortive attempts to find the true grand passion of my life, Caleb having obviously turned out something of a false alarm. A woman had to have a grand passion, I knew. I could recite one after another of the *Sonnets from the Portuguese*; and I won the National Council of Teachers of English writing award for an impromptu essay on why I would like to be Elizabeth Barrett Browning. My passion seemed long in coming, but I did not doubt its inexorable arrival.

In the meantime I had all that middle to get through. Lacking a blueprint, I improvised as best I could by scripting an endless series of obstacles that would keep me in the state of pain I could identify as love. "Love," I incanted in the hypnotic style of the diaries. "Strange word. Magic. Torture. Song. Tears." The torture and the tears were the telltale characteristics that reassured me I was where I was supposed to be. To maintain them, Caleb and I went through constant brief separations and threatened separations, little tests to prove to myself that I still couldn't live without him. During my five-month campaign I suffered without cease (my heart skipped, my hands twisted, my breath was harsh in my throat, cold sickness swept over me) and to the point of death: ". . . if he doesn't care, I'll die. I wish I were dead anyway. No, I don't. Then I couldn't be so exquisitely, painfully happy. Oh, I'm so afraid. Caleb." Within weeks of winning him, I would write, "I am so desperately confused. For so long I prayed he would love me. Now I think he does & yet I have become so terribly involved that to me the only solution is not to see each other any more. But this I cannot do, because I want him so awfully. But at the moment we are accomplishing nothing, we are clawing each other apart, & I am miserable." I made this murky rhetoric clear a few days later in an unusual burst of plaintext: "I have Caleb. And now I am petrified that I don't want him." But the next day, stricken at his failure to telephone, I wrote, "I know I love him. I am sure."

Despite my ambivalence, I made myself absolutely dependent upon him. No doubt I had read *By Love Possessed*; I was thoroughly conversant with the concept, at any rate, though nowadays I'd be more likely to think of it as *The Invasion of the Body Snatchers*. Love was something that moved in on you, took you over, made you crazy (the steps are curiously like those I traverse in a depressive episode), but you could not live without it. "I sometimes want to leave him," I wrote in February 1960, "I know I should for innumerable reasons—we do not get along, I am too moody, we are too serious, I must go to college next fall. Still, I cannot, for I find that now when I try to draw a breath without Caleb there is no air."

For someone whose greatest phobia of death is suffocation, this was a position of mortal danger. And I believed that I belonged in it, that it was a legacy of my foremothers validating my womanness. At the very beginning I wrote, "I know it is true that to a man love is just a facet of life, while to a woman it is her whole being. It is mine. My hands go automatically about their familiar tasks, entirely apart from my mind & heart & soul. I am love. My every breath depends upon Caleb, upon my loving him. If it weren't for him, I should wish to die." Months later: "We talked about college & love & aloneness. I tried to explain that today I had felt very alone when he was in that meeting because I knew that I had nothing to do with it. And that in growing up, his love for me has become only a part of his life, as it is with all men, while love is my life, as it is with all women." Now I see that the legacy comes from my forefathers, who had at least a double purpose in bequeathing it: to assure themselves of uninterrupted service from the creatures who could offer them the fullest physical and psychological comfort; and to keep those creatures so absorbed in their emotional lives that they wouldn't think to wander off and make public mischief. But the armor of this knowledge is too flimsy to protect me even today: If I am unwary enough to fall in love, my thoughts and actions start to whirl again obsessively about a dark center, a black hole, the force of gravity of which is too powerful to permit the escape even of light.

The dark center is desire, which shakes and sickens me with malarial vengeance. By the time I loved Caleb, sex and health had formed an antinomy so absolute, and desire had so disseminated itself throughout my tissues, that his very existence condemned me to chronic disease. The record of my desire is almost irretrievable, embedded as it is in a language muted by Victorian reticence ("Because it sounds so strange—almost brazen & crude—I hesitate to speak of Caleb as I feel"; "Caleb & me. As always, a strange kind of reticence keeps me from telling all about us") and composed in the lexicon of popular romance ("I turned to him fiercely, kissing him with all the pain & fear & hunger in me"). The restraint had a certain pragmatic basis. I was, after all, making a record, creating an artifact accessible to anyone who could read, and my family was highly literate. For months I debated whether or not to hide my diary, reluctant to admit a failure of trust in my mother and sister but increasingly afraid that they'd find out what I was doing. Finally I locked it into the marble-topped commode beside my bed and zipped the key into the pillow cover: "It hurts to hide," I wrote, "but I am now doing something so that I cannot look straight at the world with my head up."

And what was I doing? Moving closer and closer to doing "it." I never referred to sexual intercourse any more precisely. It was as though, forbidden the deed (and I was strictly forbidden the deed until marriage), I was also forbidden the word. "Today it almost happened." A good bit of the time, the diaries obliquely record events for which I have no images, but these images remain clear: New England in mid-April, one of the first warm days, hazy and soft. Caleb and I walk along the bridle paths deep into the woods behind my house. We lie down on the still-cool ground covered with last autumn's leaves, brown and powdery and musty now. I can feel his cock against my thigh, but my ankles are bound by my underpants so that I can't spread my knees wide enough to admit him. He butts at me ineffectively; I struggle a little as though protecting my chastity; then we give up, sit up, pull ourselves together. But a week or so later, "he asked me, though it was more of a demand than a question. I refused." I wasn't about to be humiliated by my own ineptitude again, but of course I didn't recognize that rationale. I kept the matter squarely in the moral arena: "If he needs it in two months, I promised. Is it wrong? Yes. I do not need to rationalize. I know it is wrong. And am I wicked? That I cannot answer. I know I could prevent it if I wanted to. Perhaps I will. Perhaps I won't.

Strangely enough that seems to matter very little now. It is the breaking of trust. Mama, who, I am sure, would not believe we have gone so far. God. I wish I did not have to bring religion into it, but I do. I know deeply what I should do. What will I do?" There you have her: a sixteen-year-old casuist who had already incorporated principles—both human and divine—developed in the biblical past to ensure the paternity of the highest bidder in the marital market. Unable to question those principles, even to guess that such questioning was compatible with moral survival, she could only try to come to terms with her wickedness (for, in truth, she knew the answer to that question).

Two months came and went without event, but five months later, just before leaving for college, I recorded with slightly more self-awareness, "I can hardly tell this. It is not shame I have, but I am shaken & numb. If it had not been for me, for my inability, it would have been tonight. I don't know why I could not. I was afraid, of course, but it was not really that. Caleb was rather inept, but he was good enough that he could have taken me if I'd been able, so it wasn't that either. I just did not want to. And he could not make me want to. I have no moral superstitions about evil, but I respect myself & the meaning of this act—not just as a consecration of marriage—but an expression of love which, dearly as I love him, I am not ready to give Caleb. I am relieved, of course, that it did not happen. I am concerned because it could not happen. But above all I am desperate for assurance that Caleb still loves me." Having no images for this event, I'm not sure just what caused my "inability," though I suspect my underpants once again, or maybe my hymen, which turned out to be remarkably durable.

Caleb did still love me, both longer and more deeply than I permitted myself to know. When, a couple of years later, he raped me, I was surprised. Now I am surprised only at my surprise. For one thing, he was only acting as I had long wanted him to—masterfully: "He makes me so cross & frustrated. He absolutely will, or cannot exert any influence over me. When I taunt him, I want him to shut me up, but he just takes it. I always have the feeling that I am teasing him into behaving in a strong or positive manner. And I don't want it to be like that. I want him to be firmer than I but I am afraid he isn't. Perhaps I can teach him. He needs to be taught quite a bit, I think. Not that I have had any vast experience, but I don't think he has had too much. Talk like this sounds very crude, but I must be frank with myself, if no one else. So if I can give Caleb anything he needs, I am more than willing.

But the role of teacher doesn't appeal to me. I'm too eager a student."
Still a virgin on a hot July night in 1962, I got taught.

For another, he told me he planned to have me in a letter written not
long before: "But I want this girl's ass come hell or high water. Under
the trees near the sea. Done and I'm in Valhalla." (Actually, it was done
and he was in Cairo. The next—and last—letter I got he wrote on his
way from Libya to Egypt.) I thought the letter histrionic and tossed it
aside. He was planning to take from me no more than I had once promised, of course, but at that time I believed that whatever I had come to
want everyone else must immediately want as well. For Caleb and me I
decreed friendship now instead of passionate love, and he spat on my
arrangement. In a few quick (and, as I think on it, practiced) moves, he
ensured that I could not, as he put it, "set everything in its place,"
orchestrating his emotional life to suit my emotional life. We did not
part friends.

A good feminist always hates her rapist, I suppose, but I cannot hate
mine. Not this late in my life anyway. I loved Caleb when he was little
older than my son is now, a fragile, handsome, brooding boy who
struck one pose after another, complete with British accent, German
accent, so that I was never sure who he "really" was. Being with him
was like living under one of those multifaceted silver balls that shower
light like weightless coins all over you. I was startled not long ago when
my son, helping me sort through a long-lost box of mementoes, held up
a snapshot of Caleb and asked, "Who's this? He looks dangerous." And
he did, standing in my front yard in chinos and an open-necked shirt,
brandishing a stick, his thin features, as always, unsmiling, dark shadows smudging his deep-set eyes. "That's Caleb," I told Matthew. "Oh,"
he said, "I see," knowing something of that danger. My mother, who
detested Caleb, said once that he looked like he needed a psychoanalyst, and maybe she was right. I know now that he was in trouble.
And what he didn't need was a young woman at once so self-absorbed
and so self-despising that it never occurred to her to accept responsibility for his pain, or even to credit its authenticity.

As for my own pain, it was, as I have said, all that I lived for—was,
indeed, the only way I could be sure that I was in love and therefore
alive. I let Caleb go because, ultimately, he could not hurt me anymore.
My earliest doubts about loving him are cast in just such terms: I had
gone to summer camp for a month, and when I returned I wrote, "I
wish I had not gone away & changed so greatly—I cannot remember

how it was before, exactly. Except that I loved him painfully, & now the pain is gone." To get it back, I developed painful crushes on one man after another. "It always happens," I noted at the start of one. "He is an enormously attractive man who has drawn out the need in me. Again. Again. Again I must grip the sides of the roller-coaster & scream with pleasure-pain at every dip & turn, for the ride is not fun, it is a compulsion which drags me on again for another ride of exquisite, twisting self-torture. And I can't even want to stop it." And shortly thereafter, at the start of another that would culminate in my first attempt at suicide: "Oh Adam thank you for making me alive again." Lest this lust for pain seem like mere youthful exuberance, I turn to a journal kept twenty years later: "I will not tell anyone that I am in love with a man who doesn't love me, doesn't even want me, that I am 37 years old and still getting into such a situation, that I am old and ugly and despicable and have learned nothing"; and yet "to want Richard has been a kind of resurrection, an affirmation that I am, still and after all, alive."

And so I have always been the princess in the tower, the maiden in a sleep like death in the glass coffin, waiting to be roused, waiting to be rescued. A few kisses have stirred me, but none has kept me awake for long, certainly not ever after. Yet it did not occur to me for years that the problem lay in the structural flaws in the tale itself, not in my always temporary failures to realize it perfectly. "I think I love Caleb," I wrote when I was sixteen, "I know I love him, but I cannot be sure that it is the ultimate love I am living & striving for"; "I am still searching for a love that will leave no room for doubt." I never got it.

Was I unusually stupid, to have bought the whole hog in the hope that her ears were really, in their deepest nature, silk? Considering current divorce statistics, I suspect not. Others must have succumbed to the high-pressure salesmanship in romantic expectations which teaches that a woman is an empty and idle vessel until she is filled up by "the ultimate love" for a man, and, feeling themselves go flaccid, perhaps again and again, have believed that they'd got not the wrong information but the wrong man. They must have watched the same stages in plot development—exposition, complication, climax, dénouement—build repeatedly on the screen, on the stage, on the page, without understanding that life itself takes place completely outside such a framework in a concatenation of events almost indistinguishable in their significance—washing one's hair, feeding the dog, opening the draperies in the morning and closing them at night, eating bread and

121

cheese for breakfast or for lunch or for dinner—and that no one is coming to gild these acts with glory.

At least, I didn't understand. I waited with the firmness of conviction for the "right" man, the one who could play Heathcliff to my Catherine. The men in whom I invested my hopes, in a ceaseless iteration of the self-hypnotic tale, have tended to be gentle and courtly, highly intelligent, affectionate, amusing, not much interested in mastery: rather like the image of my father I have formed from my memories and the stories I have been told. No man I have loved has ever beaten me or ordered me around; even the one who raped me did so for reasons to do less with power than with pain. All have been uneasy as objects of my obsessions and unhappy at the suffering I've gone through in order to love them. In short, as romantic heroes they have been duds, though they've been charming companions whenever I let them be.

But then, I haven't been much of a romantic heroine. I don't think that the role suits me much, or anyone else, for that matter, beyond the time it takes to read a three- or four-hundred-page novel. I've always been distractible. Even at the height of obsession, I always suspected that there were other things I might better be doing with my time; and in fact I did a great many of them, so that the whole time I was gnashing my teeth over Caleb, for instance, I was also baby-sitting, acting in high-school plays, editing the high-school literary magazine, leading Pilgrim Fellowship groups at the local and regional levels, teaching Girl Scouts to tie knots, writing term papers, sermons, letters, short stories, poems. I wish now that I'd done them more attentively, instead of through the blur of tears and terror that constituted for me the essence of life. I wish that I'd known then what I've only recently begun to know: that there is a difference between love and human sacrifice.

I feel bitter now about that waste of shame into which I have been bound as securely as signatures stitched into leather covers and into which I have drawn the other characters in my tale of woe. I despise the teachers who schooled me in principles but not the critique of principles. The protectors who wrapped my chastity so tightly in bandages of fear that I could never without torment spread my legs wide enough to let love all the way in (shame, a narrower fellow, slips in almost anywhere). The mongers of marriage, the celebrators of sorrow, the practitioners of pain, who stood me at the doorway with my little trimmed lamp and told me someone was coming when no one was coming. In short, I despise a culture that has deliberately spent my spirit so that I could not, through indiscriminate and ebullient loving, fray or rupture the ties of power—the Church over its flock, the State over its citizens, the parent over his child, the man over his woman—that keep it in place. I feel sick at the sound of my young voice bleating about Mama and God. l want to avenge the sacrifice of those two children, Caleb and Nancy, emblems of how many other sacrifices, in the service of sanctimony and superstition.

For we've paid very dearly, if not quite with our lives. For me, the price has been those recurrent attacks of love, like fits of ague racking my joints and rattling my teeth in their sockets, to escape which I have had to abandon my emotional/sexual life, and with it my body, almost entirely. For Caleb, what? Fragmented reports from friends tell of peregrinations, alcoholism, two failed marriages, a lost job. Caleb himself once called me, fifteen years after our final encounter, very drunk, and threatened to cross the country to see me, but from what I can piece together, he must have gone to a mental hospital instead. When I began to work on this essay, I suddenly grew terrified that he had died, but some distant acquaintances have reassured me that he's been dry for two years and has a job in a bookstore. I was relieved to know that he, too, was still alive, as though we were compatriots, veterans of some bitter winters-long campaign.

All the same, I was being more clever than sincere when I opened this essay with Bartleby's line. I am a spinner of stories after all, not a sorter of dead letters. I am a locus, not a terminus, of language, and what speaks me can also be spoken and, through utterance, transformed. I do bear that fatherless child in my bones, frightened, obsessed, needy, unredeemed. But the only reason that I am sitting here, at this cluttered desk in pale sunshine, drinking coffee from a brown and tan stoneware mug and smoking another cigarette, with the tabby cat under my chair and the black cat on the couch behind me, is that I was once, and thus can no longer be, that child, who never dreamed that the tale would end here.

On Living Behind Bars

In truth, the windows and doors were not barred. The windows were made of very small panes of glass sashed with heavy metal, so that although it was possible to break the glass (my friend Ed once smashed his hand through a pane, bloodying his arm from knuckles to shoulder), no opening was large enough to permit egress. The door to the ward was locked at all times, but with a doctor's permission one could get the staff to open it and thus could come and go almost at will. More important, for me at least, no one could enter the ward unless invited. Thus, the terrible, complicated, demanding world, fear of which made me flush and tremble with feverish nausea, was kept at bay. The only person who came through that door to see me was George, who arrived every night I lived there with a Brigham's chocolate ice cream soda, the only nourishment I would willingly take.

I lived for more than six months there, at Metropolitan State Hospital in Waltham, Massachusetts, most of that time on R2, the admitting ward for nonviolent patients; R3, a locked ward, was upstairs. There was also an R1, for geriatric patients, I think, and possibly an R4, but maybe I made these up. This narrative will be full of such gaps and lapses, because during the latter part of my stay my brain was zapped twenty-one times. No one seems sure how electroconvulsive therapy acts therapeutically, but everyone knows that it wreaks havoc with the short-term memory. What I have left are mostly random images, some in remarkable detail and clarity, but few embedded in any logically continuous context. I had once, many years later, a string of black clay Mexican beads on a nylon thread that snapped suddenly, in the middle of a class I was teaching, scattering little fish and birds and balls every which way. My students scrambled, retrieving many of them, and my foster son restrung them, in a new pattern necessitated by the missing pieces, into a shorter necklace. One can, to some extent, recover one's losses, but the bits that roll under the shelves, into the corners, out the door are gone for good.

I signed myself into Met State on an evening late in August 1967. Earlier in the day I had gone to my psychotherapist in a state of panic so overwhelming that I had lost all control over it. It was not a new condition—Dr. Levine had been treating me (for symptoms of depression and anxiety, I later learned) for months, as had several others before him—but by this time I was too debilitated to function at all; and he suggested that ten days of hospitalization, the standard term of commitment, might calm me enough so that I could try to resume my life. Was he lying to me? Did he know from the outset that ten days in a mental hospital, at least the first time, is only enough for coming apart altogether, and that the putting back together, if it gets done at all, will be prolonged and in some ways more dangerous than the collapse itself? Perhaps not. He can't have been many years older than I was, still in training as a psychiatrist, his head chock full of hysteria and vaginal orgasm, no doubt, and I think *he* panicked. He knew that he couldn't cope with me, that I was likely to die if left to my own devices, so he turned me over to the keepers of madwomen where whatever trouble I might cause could be closely contained.

After he, George, and I had agreed on this solution, he had some arrangements to make, so George and I left, returning later to pick up some paperwork. I think Anne may have been with us at least part of the day, but I'm not sure. She, like everyone else around me, had long since ceased to seem real; only George was left to populate my world. But I recall stopping at a park filled with play equipment which Anne particularly loved, and I don't think we'd have gone there without her. The day, hot and bright, took place in slow motion, under water. I wore flat sandals, a dress of blue cotton sprigged with lavender flowers, long-sleeved, high-waisted, and full, which my mother had made me as a maternity dress but which, thanks to the whim of fashion, remained serviceable. I cried a good deal. I knew no one who had been in a mental hospital. I couldn't believe that within a few hours I'd enter one myself. Here was failure—of nerve, of breeding—more drastic than I'd ever dreamed.

126

I was admitted to the hospital at night. I don't know why. It was a poor arrangement because it gave the whole transaction the flavor of an emergency, and I was quite panic-stricken enough without any extra theatrical effects. By this time I was sobbing reflexively, inconsolably, without cease. The admitting psychiatrist was a small Indian man (almost all the doctors there were foreigners working their way into the American system; if they were any good they quickly moved on to better hospitals or private practice). Dr. Haque. His accent was so strong that I couldn't understand most of what he said. "Why are you here? Why are you here?" he asked. I kept shaking my head and choking on tears. The silliness of this scene, both of us strangled, one on the English language and the other on grief, escaped me for several years. Before long, Dr. Haque abandoned attempts at communication, wrote several prescriptions, and sent me upstairs. An attendant locked the door behind me and set me in a chair in the small dayroom, where a number of patients were watching television. One of them asked me if I had a match and, through an oversight in security, I did. I sat among them, now dry-eyed, until someone shouted, "Meds." I queued up, as I would four times a day in the months ahead, and was given three tablets—one yellow, one blue, one white—and a little translucent green football. Then I went to bed.

~

I hadn't been able to explain to Dr. Haque what brought me to Met State, but I had no doubt that I was where I belonged. I had no doubt that I was mad. How else account for the anguish I felt in the midst of a life in every way satisfactory: marriage to an intelligent, loving man; graduation with honors from a prestigious women's college; the birth of a healthy and charming daughter; a lively job in which I'd received a significant promotion within months of my hiring. How account for the fact that I could no longer cross the threshold of my apartment without George beside me, could not swallow food in anyone's presence but George's, and not always then. Not for many years would I learn that both my situation and my symptoms made me a prime candidate for matriculation at Met State. Not for even longer would I glimpse the possibility that, though I have often been in terrible trouble, I have never been insane.

Only recently have I begun to concatenate my experiences into patterns distinct from the narrative ground in which they are embedded: This process I call essay-writing. In doing so, I have been startled at the durability of the terrible trouble I've been in. My earliest memories are anxiety-ridden: While I sit in a high chair in the kitchen of my grand-

127

mother Garm, I throw up into the dish painted with red and blue morning glories on the tray; later, I've been crying inconsolably for my lost blue blanket and a woman, Garm or perhaps her mother, Buntie, rocks me in a darkened room as I stare out into the lighted hall; my mother is nowhere around. I don't know when these incidents took place—if indeed I haven't made them up entirely—but it may have been during my three-week visit to Garm when my sister Sally was born. I was then not quite two. A few months earlier I had been hospitalized for rheumatic fever and had nearly died, not of the illness but of the sulfa used to treat me. I have no memories of this event, but it seems a likely root of the terror I felt at separation, especially from my mother. Mother herself told me not long ago of a later event—my first hysterical attack—which I also can't remember. Some time after my father's death, I suddenly asked her, in great agitation, what would become of Sally and me if she did something bad and the police took her to jail. Not all her amused assurances that she had no intention of doing anything bad, that the police didn't abscond with decent law-abiding citizens, that even if she had to go away Sally and I would be taken care of could comfort me.

As I got older, my distress grew greater, not less. The wider my horizons, the more space in my world for disaster, dreaded in the diaries I kept from the age of ten through my freshman year in college. The early diaries have disappeared, along with a string of pearls, a silver chain, my high-school yearbook, and a couple of dozen worn-out diapers I was going to use for dustrags, in one of my many moves. Thus, the first record I have of the patterns of being that would force me one day to commit myself to Met State occurs in 1957, a few months after the dissolution of my first true love affair and shortly after I entered a high school of about fifteen hundred students from a junior high of fewer than a hundred. Thrown entirely off balance, I wrote, "All is wrong. I don't understand *anything*. I'm completely upset, and tired, and numb. I hate so much, am indifferent to so much, and what love is left goes to the wrong places." I was, as usual, in the throes of an inappropriate crush: "Sometimes I wish I was still going with James. I was so happy. Now it seems I have nothing to live for except someone who doesn't live for me. Ah, my standards are all mixed up. Maybe if I understood algebra it would help. I'm bored. No, I'm just so very, very tired." I love the remark about algebra, both because it's funny and because it's true. My failure to understand algebra represented a failure to control my enlarging world, from which arose my confusion and panic, so that in a queer way my existence has been shaped by my inability to solve quadratic equations. One New Year's Eve, reflecting on the year just past, I spoke with an insight it has taken me most of the rest of my life to grasp: "I close this diary with something akin to tenderness. On its pages are the bright, happy days in my little world. And then comes the deep depression I have now, because I left this world, & it locked me out." Any transition, any separation from the past, any movement from a "little world" into a larger one resulted for me only in dread and despair.

Throughout adolescence a paradigm of living-as-illness emerged more and more clearly. For one thing, I was physically ill much of the time. Shortly after the onset of puberty I began to have migraines and disabling menstrual cramps. I also had frequent colds, which often developed into earaches, bronchitis, and febrile toxic infection. From early spring to late fall, I gasped and wept with severe hay fever. My teeth rotted, and several had to be pulled. Worst of all, because inexplicable, were the continual attacks of dizziness, nausea, and abdominal pain. By then I was already writing off my symptoms as neurotic, by which I meant something shameful and blameworthy. I must have picked the concept up somewhere in my eclectic reading, but I didn't pick up a couple of points that might have modified my self-judgmental stance: that neurotic pain hurts, and that anyone who feels ill most of the time is bound to become anxious and depressed. I simply despised myself for what I perceived as a failure of nerve (which would one day, of course, take the literal form of multiple sclerosis).

I lived in unutterable loneliness though seldom in solitude, since my family was growing with Mother's remarriage and the birth of my little brother and sister and I was heavily involved in academic and social activities. My loneliness, in fact, only grew sharper when I was in the presence of others, especially my peers. One of my earliest school memories is of my "best friend," Susan Fowler, turning on me and leading a band of children in taunting shouts—"Smitty Spider! Smitty Spider!"—the mocking of my name landing like lacerations in my flesh. From then on I felt tangential to any group, fearful of outright exclusion yet ignorant of the rules of admission, of the magic words that would let me all the way in. Gradually I learned a bit of the language, enough to pose as a member of the group, but the conflict I felt between the pose and my inward experience only increased my sense of alienation. When

I was fifteen, I came upon a passage in *Not As a Stranger*: "The discovery that it is not possible to reveal a mind to another comes early and unprotested to the majority of humans. They are reassured and protected by it. There are others to whom this discovery gives anguish. They struggle all their lives to disclose themselves." I reflected that "the passage is painfully accurate. But hasn't Merton Thompson left out another kind of person? The ones who, in disclosing themselves, mask the disclosure under a brittle sarcasm, destroying with their tongues the disclosure they desire? No, I guess he has covered everything. The latter is just a part of the poor soul who lives in the pure hell of aloneness, silence, whether imposed by self or science." By this time I believed myself isolated—permanently and through some hidden inadequacy—from the rest of humanity.

Wearing the human mask, I stumbled ahead into life, tripping time after time over my own terror. "I want so desperately to express myself," I wrote in May 1958. "I can't stand this suppression. I want to write, to act, to sing, anything. I can't. I can't." I railed against myself for being lazy and disorganized. Heartsick over my failure to have the highest marks in my class, I wrote at the beginning of 1959, "I feel so inadequate, so small," and more than a year later, "If something doesn't happen, I'll scream. I am so empty, so hungering. I know that deep within me lies something but I see it in comparison with the talents of others & it is so pitifully small." By the time I got to college, I was nearly paralyzed by dread of my inadequacy: "Why can't I study? Today I put in only 2–3 hours of studying, when 6 hours are required & I have this history exam tomorrow. I see the others buried in their books & I know I have to be like them to succeed but I don't do anything about it. I want to know but I don't want to learn. I've got to settle down or I'll not be in Wheaton long and then oh God what will become of me?"

What will become of me? What will become of me? That question grew to be the ground of my mental existence, against which the details of my joys and sorrows were picked out. And the answer was always terrible. Never mind the successes I'd had in the past (and successes did keep popping up: publications and writing awards, honor roll, acceptance into college, elected offices in school and church organizations, a long-term love affair). They were quirks of fate. I achieved each one with the last reserves of my energy and abilities. I lived at the edge of catastrophe. Certain that the next step would pitch me over, I hung back emotionally even though I took each step as it was expected of me: "I'm afraid, too, in a vague, uneasy way. Afraid of what I can do. . . . I am afraid to grow. I am afraid that when the time comes that I am grown, I will not be able to face life for fear it will not be as beautiful as it is in my private existence."

I had some inchoate sense as I was leaving for college of the way in which, as future moves through present into past, one revises the raw material into an orderly whole, but I could not yet extrapolate that the past (not to mention the present or future) is *always* purely a construct, intrinsically uninhabitable by the builder, who must live outside time in order to make time. I wanted to live in a fairy house: "Ten more days. Ten more days until I step off the edge of this bright bittersweet world into oh God into what? Surely there have been other times when I have felt like this, that I was leaving the sunny shelter of my reality to enter something inconceivable. Junior high. High school. They, dear memories, must once have been strange & frightening. But to leave, to say with finality, goodbye, old life that I have always known, goodbye house, town, family, love—oh this is pain & panic & bewilderment far wilder than I have ever known." Dragging my heels and howling like a Sabine, I inched forward into a future fraught with danger, the more so as I had to take fuller responsibility for it. "I'm scared. So constantly scared," I wrote after my first day of college classes. "I want to cry, to run from the fact that I am on my own, that everything is up to me."

Years of living in fear took their toll. I felt "sick & exhausted" all the time. By March 1958 I was recording episodes of depression, using the term in a clinically correct manner, though I would not begin to know that for another decade. "Every so often I get so deeply depressed that it is physical," I noted in June 1960. "I sit bleakly, unable to notice what goes on around me, unable to shake off a smothering apathy. . . . It is a wearing, terrifying experience." Because I could not, through strength of will or intellect, control the symptoms, I felt helpless, and I began to believe that I was going mad. In July 1959 I wrote, "The depression was worse instead of better. I suppose it is my fault. I suppose I could destroy it if I tried. But I don't know how to go about it. I just get more tense & frantic. . . . I know this sounds like a 3rd rate philosophical science fiction novel, but you have no idea what is happening to me, how near the breaking point I am. If only I did not have to live with myself, within the tortured confines of my own mind. I am going insane." And almost a year later: "I am terribly afraid of my impotence. For a while today while I was alone I thought I was dying or going insane. The depression was beyond control, pushing me to the point of panic. Now I am quieter. Yet I cannot shake this frustration."

A life of entrapment within the "tortured confines" of one's mind becomes hard to cherish. I began to long to be rid of it. Two days after my fifteenth birthday I wrote, "For the 1st time in my life I asked God to take my life & meant it." I soon made this prayer an almost daily habit. I felt helpless to sustain a life churned into ceaseless waves of pain. "Oh God I am so miserable I cannot see, I cannot think, I cannot breathe. I want to die. So many times I have wanted to die, only to find something to keep on living for until the next time life became too hard. I cannot help it. I am not fit to live. And I don't want to live. Not if it is hell like this. I want to die." As always, I perceived my choices in catastrophic terms. "I am so depressed," I wrote shortly after beginning college. "I wish I knew why so I could stop it. I'm alone & afraid always. Yet I don't know what I can do. There is no other place for me but here, & if I'm unhappy here, then I must die." Until this time death was something I awaited, a prince to wake with a kiss the sleeping beauty behind her hedge of thorns. But in December 1960 I wrote, "I wish I could break my life in half & drop it down a grate." A month after thus taking my life into my own hands, I attempted suicide for the first time. A small gesture, interrupted by the casual arrival of a friend, which left only a pale faint pucker inside my left wrist. But a quick kiss of the prince all the same.

Not long after, I stopped keeping a diary, and have kept a journal only sporadically ever since. No matter. The patterns I have just examined in some detail persisted, I know. I fell in love with a man who was willing and able to marry me, and near the end of my junior year in college we were married, but he failed to make me happy as I had expected. In my senior year, when George was away a great deal in the Navy, I consulted the college physician about my relentless anxiety. He put me on meprobamate and advised me to get pregnant (read your *Physician's Desk Reference* and then try to figure that one out), even if I had to trick George in order to do so. I took the medication, though not the advice, but it did me no good. In December 1964, in a letter I never mailed, I wrote to George, "Well, whatever the cause, I have certainly turned your life (and mine) into hell." I started psychotherapy, and I held out for rescue: "When you come home to live I hope to be a real wife again. Next summer should be good. You working like a normal person with me home keeping house." Actually the next summer was good. We were making a mutually agreed upon baby, who arrived in September. The following spring, George's stint in the Navy at an end, I went to work to put him through graduate school. A few months later I began to have agoraphobic attacks, which grew so severe that I quit work in June 1967. In August I committed myself to Met State.

But why? But why? Dr. Haque wanted to know and never found out; I'm not sure I ever spoke with him again. Once I calmed down, I thought I knew: I was crazy. I have presented my early experiences at some length, however, because I believe now that they reveal that I was not crazy at all. I never heard voices or saw visions; I never confabulated; my affect, though often mournful, was never inappropriate; I often wished but never believed myself someone else; I never feared that objects or people were trying to harm me; I was neither violent and abusive nor totally withdrawn. My failure was not in perceiving reality: I perceived it full well, and despised it. In it my father was dead, friendships were difficult and romances impossible to sustain, my efforts at writing were clumsy, and each day was pretty well indistinguishable from every other. Life was a ramshackle structure, and I was a painstaking architect with outraged sensibilities.

Such a person is not mad, though she may, as I did, take to scribbling. The raw materials of my life seemed sluggish, entropic, and I labored to give them definition. Hence the diaries, I think, though I didn't understand their function at the time. In fact, it seems not to have occurred to me that I was writing my life until shortly after that first suicide attempt, when my college roommate commanded me to stop living in a dream world and I reflected, "Poo is right about the dream world. I don't know when it started—the game which is a constant story. I don't think I have been without it since we got back from the tropics. I seem always to have lived in my imagination. At first I suppose it was just for pleasure; then it became a habit, a way of living. Now everything I see or experience becomes part of a pattern. It is rather a beautiful way to live, for I am acutely sensitive to the things I hear or see or do, to moods & colors & perceptions. Perhaps that is why I don't want to move out of it." Here was a potentially useful insight into my existential mode, but with the same breath I reached it I judged and rejected it: "But lately I have been so afraid that I know it is a torturous way to live also. It's dangerous to live alone in a pleasant world of shadows, unaware of unpleasantness. Not that I don't know that ugliness & pain & hate exist, for I have seen them and felt them. It is just that, finding them insupportable, I exclude them, replacing them with my own unreality which has begun to haunt me. It has made me self-centered, over-dramatic, callous to others. Yet even tho' I see these things, I don't know whether I'll be able to leave it. I've got to try, tho'—I've got to try to save my life."

Clearly I believed that the "dream world" was in every way *separate from* "reality" instead of *constituting* my reality, all that I would ever get. I saw two worlds, the "wrong" one in which I lived and the "right" one occupied by everyone else, and I battered my fists and face and knees trying to break through from one to the other. The "right" world was a mirror trick, of course, a true dream world, played by a culture that creates and then taunts outsiders: "Smitty Spider! Smitty Spider!" I really had no place else to go. Thus, in order to "save" my life I could only leave it. The paradox was insoluble.

I went to Met State to get cured not of madness but of being me.

~

If in fact I was, as I now believe, not crazy but a sort of cultural prisoner, Met State certainly made a madwoman of me. The label realizes the condition: Call a woman crazy, and she'll justify your faith. Especially if you lock her into a drab and dirty space with dozens of other wayward souls, make sure that she is never alone, feed her oatmeal and bananas until her bowels are starched solid, drug her to the eyeballs so that she can scarcely read or speak, and threaten to shoot bolts of electricity through her brain.

Met State may have been, as reputed, the best of the state hospitals in Massachusetts. It was not a good place. I spent most of my sojourn on the "best" ward, the one for short-term patients. Located on the second floor of a modern box of brick, it contained sleeping wings for men and for women, made up of several pavilions of four beds each separated by chest-high partitions, as well as a laundry room, a shower room, and a toilet room. The three toilets had neither seats nor handles; one squated over them, then flushed by pressing a button. They were separated only by low partitions with no doors. Men, I suppose, grow used to communal elimination, but I never did.

134 Between the sleeping wings was a common area holding two recreation rooms, one large and one small, the meds station, and a cafeteria-style dining room. We were discouraged from crawling into our beds

during the day, so I spent most of my time in the large recreation room, staring out of the small-paned windows at the green, then gold, then brown, then white of the wide hospital grounds. I was so heavily drugged, especially at the beginning when I was being given anti-psychotics, that I couldn't read or write much, but I worked on an intricate piece of crewel embroidery some of the time, and listened to the Red Sox in the World Series on a tiny portable radio with an ear plug. Every time the Sox made a good play, I clapped in glee, and since the radio was all but invisible in my lap, I suppose that my outbursts complicated my psychiatric diagnosis. Three times a day I was forced into the dining room, but I couldn't swallow food when people were around, so I ate almost nothing and lost weight steadily. When I got down to ninety-three pounds, I was given the choice of being put onto the medical ward for intravenous feeding or taking a horrid, lumpy dietary supplement, like liquid oatmeal, called Liprotein, which I was promised I could drink alone. I was still made to go to meals, but after each one I was escorted into the laundry and left with my Liprotein.

The ten days of my voluntary commitment came and went, and I signed a new form, for an indefinite time. I had yet to see a doctor, though I did attend a couple of sessions of group therapy, which left me frightened and upset. Dr. Levine came once, but I felt too panicky to talk to him, and he never returned. Finally, on the eighth of September, I was assigned to Dr. Julian, an Austrian woman. I refused to see her ("Not sure why—," I jotted in the journal I'd begun to keep erratically, "don't want to be intimate with a woman, perhaps"), and wound up being carried into her office because I wouldn't walk, but once there I found her "tough and perceptive and intelligent." Today I can hardly remember her, but she worked with me regularly, and occasionally also with George, and I suppose that she saved my life, a gift for which I have sometimes been grateful.

Shortly thereafter I was given a battery of tests—IQ, TAT, Rorschach—perhaps on Dr. Julian's orders. I don't know why. No one ever explained any aspect of my condition to me. At the time I took the tests, I was very disheartened about my lack of progress, and my discouragement made me sullen and uncooperative. My responses were terse and disjointed. A few days later another psychiatrist, also a woman, came to the ward to tell me that I was schizophrenic and would have to have insulin-shock therapy. I knew about insulin shock. My grandmother had died in a diabetic coma. And the patients under treatment were housed on R2 because they needed constant supervision. They disappeared each morning. When they returned they sat drowsily in their bathrobes, sipping chocolate milk heavily sweetened with corn syrup. Every so often one would nod off, and then their nurse would slap her face and shout at her until she roused. They were as fat as slugs, as slow, almost as silent. And the treatment lasted months. I had come for a few days, and now I was to be incarcerated for months. At the risk of being thought crazier than ever, I threw a fit.

Dr. Julian was furious when she heard what had happened. She assured me that the tests had not revealed schizophrenia and that she would never permit me to be treated with insulin shock. She was true to her word. She wanted me instead to have electroconvulsive therapy. I wasn't much happier with that suggestion. I refused to sign the necessary paper, and we reached a stalemate.

For the first month or so, I never left the ward, though I was soon permitted to do so, except accompanied by George for awkward visits home. In late September the whole ward was herded out for a picnic, and in my journal I recorded, "I didn't want to go, but I did go. Terribly anxious at first, then calm enough to eat a hot dog, finally enjoying lying alone on the grass in the sun." Wearing a black turtleneck and yellow jeans printed with tiny red and black flowers, I lay in the last of the summer's heat, belly full, in a brief moment of ease. "Maybe I'll try to go out a bit from now on," I wrote that night. And thanks to a new companion, I did start leaving the ward.

At this point I did something so predictable that I can almost (but only almost, mind you, only almost) laugh at it: I fell in love with one of the other inmates, a young man named Ed who was part of the emerging drug culture. On R2 about half of us were under twenty-five, and of that number I was the only one who had never done any drugs, except alcohol and the pills in the little paper cups that were handed to me four times a day. Part of the reason I fell in love with Ed was that I was lonely and bored. I had always vaguely thought that it was the brilliant who were unstable, especially artists, of which I had once fancied myself one; and perhaps if I'd gone to McLean Hospital, the elegant buildings and grounds of which I could glimpse on the next hill, with the likes of Robert Lowell and Sylvia Plath, my glamorous fantasy would have been validated. But at Met State I learned about the tedium of madness: "It's that there's no one here to talk with intelligently. Each patient has a theme that is repeated over and over—Ruth bragging about her cleaning, her house, her ability to earn money as a waitress, all in loud, rough, ungrammatical language; Anne preaching Holy Roller religion; Muriel complaining that someone disturbed her sleep; etc., etc. I'm sick of it. It didn't matter at 1st—everything was new and strange then, and I didn't pay much attention to others anyway." The men were no more promising companions: John, a big soft boy terrified that he was gay, who was himself some days, dressed in jeans and an oxford-cloth shirt, and others was Jesus Christ, naked but for one of the striped spreads that covered all our beds; David, who had been in mental institutions since he was four, rocking and humming and flapping one hand in front of his face for hours on end; sweet Homer, a small round grey man in his fifties who yearned wistfully and fixedly for death as for a beautiful woman. Ed was intelligent, educated, usually lucid. He liked to write poetry and to listen to music. I tried to attract him, I noted, "telling myself the whole time, of course, that I wasn't doing any such thing. Because I'm not sure I want him. It seems sometimes like an exercise, a test of my charm, and something to do during these long, boring days."

But I also fell in love with him because being "in love" was, as it had always been, the only condition that promised me any hope of rescue from myself: "The effect is, at least, exhilarating. I feel more alive, more in touch than I have in a while." I was by this time drowning in domesticity. "Me home keeping house" hadn't turned out to be what I needed after all, and getting a job had only exacerbated my situation by providing one more arena for potential failure. "I have the feeling that Dr. Julian and George and everyone who's trying to 'help' is just cramming a way of life down my throat," I wrote. "I'm not sure I want it—to be sober and stolid and settled. I like to play. I want to play. What a drag the real world seems. Full of dust rags and shrieking babies, of meals to cook, evenings of bridge with nice young couples. Ugh." No wonder my throat tightened and my stomach heaved in the face of food. I couldn't swallow anything more.

With Ed I played: two irresponsible loonies in a legally drugged haze. We listened to Tim Buckley and The Beatles' "Magical Mystery Tour" and the Jefferson Airplane on the ward's tinny portable phonograph. We wandered for hours hand in hand around the hospital grounds. We headed into the woods and made love. One afternoon I remember going to my bed, taking off my underclothes and knit stockings, pulling on my woolen coat with muted green and purple stripes

137

known in my family as the horse blanket, all under the sour suspicious gaze of a woman in a nearby bed, then running bare-legged from the ward into the woods to meet Ed and fall onto a snow-covered heap of leaves in a clumsy, shivering embrace. For some reason, this really did seem better than the "real world" of warm wide beds.

We did one another no good, of course, and possibly a fair amount of harm. I think now that I prolonged my stay because I was too obsessed to leave him. Toward the end, when I went home on a trial basis, I returned after five days "suffering attacks of nausea, unpredictable and unmanageable." As soon as I saw Ed again, "I nearly fainted. The old romantic swoon. The gladness at being with him again, at finding him happy to see me—it's so powerful. But so are the fear and sadness and despair. And I suspect that they are very important to me. It's been so long since I really suffered in love. And as Ed pointed out in group meeting this morning, sadness can be in a strange way enjoyable—it can be creative, productive." The old romantic swoon indeed. The old romantic swindle. And I was still buying whatever shares came on the market.

Despite my claims of exhilaration and happiness after I met Ed, my condition continued to deteriorate, though not visibly, I assume, since some time late in October I was allowed to make plans for leaving the hospital. I drove into Cambridge one day to ask Mr. Tillinghast, my boss at the Smithsonian Astrophysical Observatory, if I could return to work. He accepted me warmly. In a seamless movement I then drove home instead of back to Met State. In the bathroom I stood in front of the marble sink and swallowed one Darvon after another. When I had taken them all, I drove back to the hospital, undressed, and got into bed. Just before drifting off, I recall telling another patient what I had done. I came to the next morning in the Intensive Care Unit of the Waltham City Hospital, lungs aflame from a bronchoscopy necessitated by my aspirating vomit while unconscious, wired like the Bride of Frankenstein. In a while I was moved to a regular room, and a couple of days later I went back to Met State in an ambulance. The men who drove were glad to see me and praised the improvement in my looks. I didn't remember them from my earlier ride, but I was touched that they were clearly happy that I hadn't died.

138

The next entry in my journal, headed simply "Monday," begins, "I don't know the date. I've been here so long now. Summer has gone and much of autumn. The weather is cold enough that Anne needs her snowsuit." A little further on, "There's much more to me than I knew.

And the parts that I didn't know are the ones on top now, coming out strangely, controlling me. It's still *me*, I'm sure, no one else, but I don't know this person. I'm not frightened, am I? I guess I am. I surely must know of what; they keep asking what? what? what? I feel crazy now. I've never been crazy before. I wish I were dead." The following one, dated 7 November, restates my dread: "I'm not at all dead. But I'm so afraid that I'm going mad. I've had a lot of medicine, so it's probably just that. I hope. I wonder if Dr. Julian would let me go mad. I wonder if she could stop me."

She certainly wanted to stop me, and she continued to insist that shock treatments would help, but I still refused. Late in November, she transferred me to Continuing Therapy and Guidance—CTG—the wonderfully euphemistic title of the heart of Met State, the chronic wards, which held seven hundred men and seven hundred women with one psychiatrist for each sex. I lasted there about a week. Then I revolted. "I mean to leave this place," I wrote. "It is unbelievably dismal—and I'm on the *best* ward in CTG. There is everywhere a sense of age and decrepitude about both the buildings and the patients. Everywhere grime and the sour stench of sweat and urine. The 'day room' is a wide hall littered with old, garishly painted Windsor chairs and lit by a few low-watt bulbs. At night nowhere in the ward is there light enough to read by. I sleep in a large dormitory with about 16 beds—the bed sags and groans with the slightest movement. Worst of all are the meals, served in a cavernous dining hall reached by a circuitous route I still haven't figured out. No question of eating in those surroundings. So I am in every sense uncomfortable—sleepless, hungry, and oppressed.

"I do not believe that this is 'better' for me than R2; and I don't think the whole damned hospital is doing me much good. I'll ask Julian this afternoon to make me a day patient; if she won't, I'll try to sign myself out. I'll admit to being frightened, but also eager to show some initiative."

I know now that Dr. Julian had done just what she set out to do: to scare the wits out of me. She agreed instantly to my becoming a day patient. My rapid departure from CTG was something of a miracle: The shortest stay I heard of while there was that of a young woman who'd been there two years, the next shortest, of a man who'd been there six. I found that I had limits to what I'd do, even for craziness. I bolted.

139

Within two weeks I failed as a day patient, disintegrating into "unbearable depression. Indescribable really. I can only say that I now know what it is like to exist from minute to minute—and that just barely. Tonight, free of it, I find myself praying that I shall never go there again." Now, as Dr. Julian must have known, I had reached a crux: I could either kill myself, as I had demonstrated, or return to the dim halls of CTG. Once again she offered me shock treatment. I signed the papers without hesitation and returned to R2.

Between the middle of December and the middle of February I had twenty-one treatments, at the rate of three, two, and then one a week. They were painless yet vaguely dreadful. Each time, my fluid intake was restricted and I was given shots to dry up my secretions and relax my muscles. With a group I was led downstairs; we waited lined up on straight chairs in the dim light behind screens until our names were called one at a time. When I heard mine, I walked around the screens and lay on a bed while a nurse jabbed sodium amytal into my arm. Almost immediately, lovely waves of sleep, later groggy consciousness, finally a reward of dessert and coffee. Sometimes I had a headache, but otherwise felt no physical effects.

Mentally I felt very peculiar. "I feel as tho' I am in a dream," I wrote after the second treatment; a month later, "I feel very strange the last couple of days—things even smell funny to me"; a few days after that, "I have gone as mad as a hatter. I don't know what has happened. But for several days now I have felt really crazy. And badly frightened." But on the twenty-eighth of January I wrote, "Sitting here this morning, I suddenly felt stronger and more competent than I have been feeling. Perhaps one day I will be capable of handling life on the outside by myself," and on the eighth of February I recorded that I weighed a hundred eight pounds. I began to go home for a few hours each evening; I invited my sister and her husband to dinner; on the eleventh of February George and I went to a movie; I spent one day at home with Anne on my own, then two. On the twenty-third I went home "for as long as I want," and although I fled back to the hospital after five days, I didn't stay long. The next time I left, I didn't return.

~

Much earlier, I referred to myself as a "cultural prisoner" in Met State. If that phrase is to be more than radical rhetoric, then I must confront and explore the terms of my incarceration. I do not believe that I was not "sick" at the time I was locked up, or even necessarily that I was badly treated while I was there. On the contrary, today I believe in my illness more purely as illness—rather than mental weakness or moral flaw—than I could ever have done then; and since I left the hospital after only six months, my treatment seems to have been unusually effective in view of the rather primitive conditions under which it took place. I was sick, all right, but what I see now is that sickness forms only in relation to some standard of health which does not exist of itself in some fictional objective other world but which is created from the observations, responses, values, and beliefs of those "healthy" subjects who seek to articulate it. If every human being, for instance, formed patches of plaque in his or her central nervous system, then I would not have multiple sclerosis; I would be normal and those without sclerotic spots (should they be so lucky) would be aberrant. The example is extreme, perhaps, but it holds this grain of truth: that the standards of social, moral, and emotional health in a patriarchal culture are so set (whether by those with sclerotic patches or those without is moot but bears investigation) that for a woman sickness may be intrinsic to her existence.

Dr. Julian told me that my "life became troubled when men entered it," and I accepted her Freudian-tinged explanation at its face value: that I had failed to adapt my personal existence to the presence of James and Fred and Caleb and Adam and George and Ed in it. I did not think of my experiences as in any way typical rather than idiosyncratic; and I never believed my responses to them anything but problematic. The possibility that those responses, though maladaptive, might have been in a curious way the saving of me—the life ring that kept me from going down in a sea of womanly graces—I have only just begun to explore.

Indeed my life became troubled, not when individual men entered it, but when I emerged from the long undifferentiated dream of my female-supported childhood into the Real/Male World, an environment defined and dominated by the masculine principles of effectiveness, power, and success, an environment containing a ready-made niche for me which happened to be the wrong size and shape. Some days I longed to smash the entire hideous alien structure, but I had no tools. Other days I wanted nothing more than to fit into my niche, even if I had to whack off my hands and my feet and my head to do so. Empty-handed, contemplating self-mutilation, of course I grew depressed. I believe now that my depression was—and still is—my response to the struggle not to go under, not to go down for the last time, sinking into acceptance of that space which crabbed and cramped me. I will not be the little woman, my depression cried, even while I was hunching and squeezing, cracking my bones and scraping my knuckles and knees. I will die first. For this reason I call it the saving of me.

It was not entirely coincidental, I suppose, that my depression grew prominent after my mother remarried when I was eleven. Then, for the first time in seven years, a man literally entered my life to stay, though he did so with exceptional gentleness. My stepfather's rare calm, together with his capacity for accepting and cherishing people just as they are, certainly eased the upheaval his sudden presence caused. Even so, he separated my mother from me, calling from her a new kind of attention. And through her experiences I observed the contours of a grown woman's life up close. She quit her part-time job at Stepping Stones School for Exceptional Children. And then she made babies: Nathan and Barbara. I adored the babies, who came at just the right time to thrill me to my early-adolescent core. But I must have found their effects on Mother tiresome, for I remember complaining to Aunt Jean while visiting her in the Boston house, which was filled with books and modern paintings, not to mention writers and musicians and curious strays both human and feline, that I was sick of conversations about diapers and feedings.

I both wanted and didn't want the normalcy my mother's new life conferred. As soon as I began to perceive the traits of a womanly existence, I longed for them: "I want to be normal. Not average, normal. I want to be witty & charming & *popular,* especially with boys. I don't want to be different." Yet I relentlessly subverted my own desires: "I have no one to talk to. Sometimes I know I am aloof, but I'm not stuck-up. It's just that I have too much to think about. I don't want to think about clothes and boys. What's wrong with me?" A couple of years later I seem to have improved my conversational techniques, though without increasing my satisfaction: "I am easier with the kids now—I can joke with them & chat informally. But always I feel so isolated, so awkward, so alone." Uneasy among my peers, I groped for friendship with older women, like my drama coach. "I try—I really think I do try to be close to the kids my own age," I reflected. "It is no good. I am awkward & uncertain. With Miss Hare it is different. I am still very young & ungainly but it is not so important that I do not say what I am expected or do the logical thing. I can be me—sulky if I want, or blithe; temperamental or gay or pensive. There is not the same pressure to be typical." But of course such relationships—pashes, I think the British call them—were too unequal to erase my loneliness.

I finally found out what was "wrong" with me years and years later in a conversation with my present therapist. I had been bemoaning—still—my inability to make friends when Ken asked me how I had liked to spend my time when I was young. After I described, with considerable enthusiasm, the long walks I took in all weathers through the woods behind my house, he said, "There's a term for people like you." "What?" I perked up, always eager to pick up a new bit of psychological jargon. "It's called being introverted," he said. Introverted, for God's sake. Some new jargon. Yet, familiar though the word was, I'd never applied it to myself. And suddenly, trying it on, I understood that my loneliness was not an aberration but an existential choice. "I think I *ought* to want friends," I jotted in my journal after our conversation. "But by and large people don't exist for me unless they're present or built into my interior landscape. And I certainly don't want to spend time with them."

Introversion is no illness. It's simply a habit of mind. Why then did I view it as the doom of my happiness and fulfillment? I could have done so only by believing that the one avenue to that happiness and fulfillment was laid not with my own insights and actions but with my relationships to others. And there, of course, is the paving stone of a womanly existence: to create and elaborate the social bonds that sustain community. Church fairs. Choir picnics. PTA. Summer playground programs. Covered-dish suppers. Christmas pageants. The men may leave the community regularly—in a village the size of the one I grew up in, all but a handful had to work elsewhere—but they leave their women behind with their telephones and their morning coffees and their bridge luncheons and their afternoon teas, all talking a mile a minute, their words like needles and patches and thread, their lives one long quilting bee of human bonding. Gossip is not idle. It is an exercise in design, the picking out of patterns in the social fabric. The fingers of every woman strengthen and embellish the whole.

A woman clumsy with a needle can thus be a serious liability, as can one who shirks the task. I kept meandering off, both literally, on those long solitary wooded ambles, and figuratively, plunging into inward thickets because I had "too much to think about." My mother moderated and socialized my behavior as best she could. She frowned at, though she did not forbid, my jaunts. She paid for, though she could ill

143

afford, ballroom-dancing lessons, summer camp, Fellowship retreats. She discouraged those too-passionate single attachments I formed desperately time and again, those fascinations with one other which disrupt the warp and woof of social intercourse. Instead she approved of group activities, and these I plowed into compulsively, taking on more and more responsibility, until the race from stage to printer to pulpit to meeting hall left me more than half dead with exhaustion.

None of this gave me any less to think about, only less time in which to do the thinking. Why then did I do it? I was a genuinely good child, a typical first-child/girl, who liked to please others. Too, my mother conveyed to me, for the most part tacitly, that my natural way of being—solemn, solitary, reflective—was neither wholesome nor attractive; and my experience certainly bore her out. I was in a hopeless bind: to do as I would—to please others—I could not be as I was. And the greed for thinking: What does that signify? Simply, I think now, that I was a writer, which is not so dreadful a fate when you think about some of its alternatives. I could, for example, have been a certified public accountant. But from this distance I can see that, for that girl in that small town in the late 1950s, it set up some insoluble conflicts that turned it into quite a dreadful fate indeed.

I loved to write. I squeezed as much scribbling as I could into my exhaustingly sociable schedule. I felt driven to it. "I want to write," I began a passage of rhetoric so mushy that it recently collapsed my daughter (who, though not much older than I was when I wrote it, seems curiously unsympathetic to my adolescent quirks) into unseemly hoots. "I want to create, to create the world I love, a world intense in its vagueness, vivid in its non-existence. I want to give to others who may need it what I live on—dreams, imaginations, in forms so real they vibrate. I want to create for them people I know, who are alive just across the border. The border between this and that."

It was in this yearning that I located—probably pretty accurately—that difference which generated my isolation. Do others, I wondered, "see things as I do? I do not think so, for if they did they would not still be alive." And, lifethreatening though my vision seemed, I would not repudiate it: "Sometimes I think I shall die from being different even as I cling to the difference fiercely." In short, I believed myself—not unusually for an adolescent—possessed of a special gift that could transform life from the drudgery of French assignments and allergy shots and arguments with my disappointingly ordinary boyfriend into a valiant quest: "Sometimes, vaguely, in the murkiness which is my mind, my creativity, my genius, flashes a glimpse of this greatness which is pure pain & pure joy. Yet I do not know what it is or where to find it. I do know this—that when I find it, if I find it, I will discard all else as meaningless & follow it for the rest of my life." Out of the kitchen and onto the steed.

But I never made it. I never became a writer. Instead I became The Gifted Girl with Lots of Potential, as I christened her twenty years and more later. I never got one foot into the stirrup, let alone sat astride the beast. And because I failed to do so, I almost died of sorrow.

I believed my failure the result of my personal shortcomings. The gift was simply not good enough. "I know that deep within me lies something," I had written, "but I see it in comparison with the talents of others & it is so pitifully small." After typing up some poems, I commented, "It is disheartening that so few have the slightest merit. But some show what I hope is promise." I didn't much believe in the promise, though. Once when my sister took some of my poems, changed their dates, and signed her name to them behind my back, I could summon no outrage but only a verbal shrug: "I don't much care. They aren't any good anyway." And they weren't, of course. I've still got a sheaf of them, and they're dreadful drivel. What else does a fifteen-year-old write? But I couldn't forgive myself for being fifteen. A voracious and catholic reader, I was steeped in the mature work of hundreds of writers, and I knew—I was not a stupid reader—that mine didn't come anywhere near the mark.

Much more damaging than my disgust at my work, however, was my self-repugnance. The gift might be pitifully small, but worse yet, I failed to use it. "Something in me is crying out," I wrote. "The desire to create. I cannot. My brain is frayed with the need to produce, but I am paralyzed. I keep saying—when I have time. Yet when I do have a free moment, I waste it. I feel pent up, desperate. My ability rides me. My lack of it tortures me. I am torn apart." This paralysis would lie at the core of my depression ever after. But I now think it worthwhile to look at the context in which I wrote that passage, because it reveals not a lazy wastrel, as I believed, but a woman trapped in the manifold webs of female duty and expectation.

I had just graduated from high school and planned to go to a very expensive college in the fall, so I had to go to work for the first time in my life. Since my only experience was baby-sitting, I logically took a job as a mother's helper for an affluent couple with three small children. The woman was a version of what I would become in a few years, all resentment and raw nerves; her particular fixation (rather different from mine) was cleanliness. Every day I washed floors, vacuumed and dusted, did mountains of laundry (no towel could be used twice, and the children had to have clean clothes three times a day) and ironed it all, even the children's T-shirts and the man's boxer shorts. I also attended the children, of course, and since I wasn't allowed to leave them for a moment, I had to postpone many chores till after they were asleep. I tumbled exhausted each night into a cot in the baby's room and woke with him each morning at 5:30. In short, I was initiated into female adulthood with a rigor that made my mother's efforts in this direction seem feeble. To make matters worse, I was bitterly homesick, fearful of going to college, and lonely for my boyfriend, who'd gone on a cross-country camping trip. In this setting, depleted both physically and emotionally, I flagellated myself for failing to create. As well ask poetry of a paper bag.

And yet, when the time came three years later, I chose the depletion rather than the poetry. Unable to believe in greatness, I could not discard all else as meaningless and follow it for the rest of my life. On the contrary, I discarded greatness as meaningless and opted for a man and his child. That I was miserable in marriage and motherhood did not reflect on my choice. It merely indicated that something was still—interminably—wrong with me. So wrong that at last I had to go to the hospital to get fixed.

My choice did not change while I was there. Only once in my hospital journal did I mention writing, toward the end of my stay: "I can't write poetry. I'm afraid I'll never be able to." My concern was not with writing but with relationships, especially my relationships with George and Anne. Indeed, I can trace the progress of my therapy and my satisfaction with it through my attitude toward Anne and my duties to her. Early on, in reflecting about her, I grasped and stated my central problem: "I want to see her but I don't want to take care of her. I wonder if I want her at all in any adult fashion. I'm not very grown up."

I certainly wasn't very grown up. Transitions had always been problematic for me, remember. When I was fifteen I had written, "I'm afraid to grow. I am afraid that when the time comes that I am grown, I will not be able to face life for fear it will not be so beautiful as it is in my private existence." And I'd sure as hell been right. The transition into female adulthood had been impossible. Thinking back on that summer as a mother's helper, I'm not exactly surprised. So the task I set for myself while I was at Met State was to turn myself into a grown woman; and the gauge of my maturity was my ability to want to mother my daughter.

It wasn't easy. "It seems unspeakable that I should not want and love my child," I wrote. "But she seems to represent to me everything I rebel against—being tied to the house, following dull routine, and above all accepting responsibility." Getting well to me meant ending my rebellion. Gradually I yearned to do so: "I feel so sad—especially toward Anne. I miss her so and feel so ashamed that I can't take care of her like a real mother. She is beautiful, so sweet and bright. Why can't I be an ordinary woman. We visited the Maxons on Saturday and I envied Judy bitterly—caring for David, keeping her own house, ready to have another baby. I want to be like that." And "I want to be well. I want to be like Sally, like Judy, like my mother. Not that they are living in a state of bliss—that would be a drag, I should think. But they cope with their lives and get joy out of them. I should be able to do that, too. I have everything going for me—intelligence; education; a loving, understanding, patient husband; a bright, charming daughter. Why am I sick and frightened? How can I get well?" And "I would give almost anything to be Judy Maxon, settled in her ordinary little ranch house, busy with her 2 little children, etc." Finally, "I miss George and Anne so much. Even tho' yesterday was frightening and exhausting, it was promising. I want to live at home. I want to be well." Shortly thereafter I went home to live.

~

I did not, however, get well. I got functional, which is another condition altogether (though not, on the whole, one to be sneezed at). My ignorance of the difference, which almost cost me my life, I attribute to my doctors, none of whom taught me the first thing about depression. Not one told me that I had quite a common illness, of which disrupted sleeping patterns and loss of weight are clear-cut symptoms, and which tends to respond readily to drug therapy. When, after my release from the hospital, I fretted to Dr. Levine about a possible recurrence, he assured me that there was no reason to believe that I would ever have one. I suppose he was adopting the typical medical stance, especially toward hysterical females: If you tell them about a symptom, they're sure to develop it, so the less said the better. He'd have done me better service to warn me that nearly half the people who experience one depressive episode will experience another, and that as a woman I was at an especially high risk. Instead, he gave me to believe that I'd paid my dues and could now get on with my life.

I never did go back to the hospital, at least. In that escape I was luckier than most women at Met State. Agnes had come back, leaving her year-old baby and several other children, for her fourth series of shock treatments. Shelly, who had slid from McLean down to Met State when the frequency of her hospitalizations became too expensive even for her advertising-executive husband, tallied and recounted her suicide attempts with rhapsodic vigor. Their families had evolved systems for accommodating mother's absence with as little disruption as feasible. And then there were those seven hundred women in CTG, many of whom had lived longer at Met State than anywhere else, with their faded hair and eyes, shuffling through the dim corridors in soft house slippers, fingers plucking at the pale flowers on their limp cotton shifts. Their families, if they had any, must long since have grown disheartened, perhaps even moved away, for no one ever came for them. In any case, the incarceration of these women became a structural component—whether as presence or as absence—in the lives connected with theirs. Mine never did.

One of my greatest fears about having been hospitalized was that I'd never be given a job again. But in truth I found my re-entry into the world remarkably easy. Shortly after my suicide attempt, I had a note from my boss at the Smithsonian Astrophysical Observatory: "Please don't worry about your job at SAO. I think it will be here when you get back. Come when you're ready. I can always use your kind of help. If you want, you can try a little part-time work later on. Remember that, while I appreciate your responsible attitude, it won't matter if you miss an occasional appointment here." This calm man, who would be dead himself within a couple of years at the age of thirty-six of lung cancer, rescued my shambled life. Shortly after my release I did go back, at first part-time, soon full-time. I discovered then that Mr. Tillinghast had never accepted my resignation but had put me on leave without pay, so that my service was continuous and there's no awkward gap in my résumé.

In fact, however, I've never had to conceal that gap. From the beginning I've been able to tell people about my hospitalization without catastrophe. I've encountered puzzlement, even skepticism—after all, when you meet me, in my conservative clothes, with my face carefully made up, wearing the poise bequeathed me by my paternal grandmother, you're more likely to think you're seeing Mrs. Middle America than a madwoman, though in truth Mrs. Middle America is, very often, a madwoman—but seldom suspicion and never rejection. I've never been denied anything I wanted on the grounds of mental instability. In this I am no doubt fortunate, ironically, in being female. Women, because they have been viewed by their culture, embodied in the last century or so not in priests but in scientists, especially psychologists, as deviating from the white male bourgeois norm that culture imposes, have been permitted, indeed expected, to manifest a certain amount of mental and emotional dis-ease. So six months in a mental hospital in an odd way has rendered me normal. Too, I never tried to do anything my culture considers particularly responsible. I worked at low-paying jobs without authority in nonprofit organizations, and I confined myself to culturally devalued activities. Child-rearing, editing, writing, teaching: What real harm could I do? No one had to force me, as they did Thomas Eagleton in 1972, to withdraw from candidacy for vice president of the United States because I'd been treated in a mental hospital for depression.

And yet, though I learned to function, however modestly, on "the outside," as we used to call it in the hospital, I never got well. I didn't know that I was still depressed. Remember, no one had ever taught me about depression, so I came to associate it with the episode that put me into the hospital. I didn't know that it could, in its chronic permutation, twist itself into the fibers of my existence, a continuous strand of unusual tensility so woven into my way of looking at the world as to constitute, together with the greyish cast of my eyes and my laboring limp and my fondness for Reese's Peanut Butter Cups and my fear of all spiders except tarantulas, my self. Maggie Scarf in *Unfinished Business: Pressure Points in the Lives of Women* suggests that my depression might really be analogous to my eye color, that is, that it has a genetic basis. Depressive episodes are often triggered by ruptures in relationships, and females appear from the moment of birth to form, sustain, and rely upon relationships more readily than males; thus, she reasons, females are genetically predisposed toward relatedness as one of the species' survival mechanisms, and consequently predisposed as well toward depression.

Until a relational and/or depressive gene is discovered, I remain skeptical about such an explanation, smacking as it does of the biological determinism which has forced women to bear children because they have the necessary equipment, telling them that they must fulfill their maternal instinct (as Betty Rollin points out in "Motherhood: Who Needs It?" an instinct is something you die from not obeying, and no woman has ever died from not having a baby, though plenty have died in childbirth); and which has forbidden them education because their brains are too small, telling them that knowledge leads to madness. But I don't think we need such a gene anyway. Acculturation is quite powerful enough to emplace the parameters that will yield, time after time, female derangement. I do not deny, however, that depression, whatever its etiology, manifests a physiological component, most often in eating and sleeping disorders that, because they are clearly controlled with medication, suggest some sort of biochemical imbalance in the depressive's system.

In the summer of 1980, almost exactly thirteen years after my commitment to Met State, I slid precipitously into another acute depressive episode. Because I had not understood that I could have such a breakdown again, I did not recognize what was happening to me, and by the time one of my neurologists did, it was almost too late. I took the antidepressant medication he gave me all at once instead of in the measured doses he'd prescribed. I was lucky that the psychiatrist who interviewed me in the emergency room chose to send me home rather than commit me to the hospital, because I think, on the basis of my earlier experience, that in the hospital I'd have gotten much worse before I began to get better. As it was, I had a pretty bad time of it for a few months, but I survived intact.

And at last I began to learn about depresssion. I had, finally, a therapist who was willing to teach me and also to be taught by me as I began to explore the significance of my illness, and who could see that, even though I was a woman, my adjustment to marriage and motherhood was not, somehow, quite the point. I turned back and back into my experience, not to seek the origins of my illness in that experience, because I had stopped believing that any event or series of events had made me sick, but to find the structure of my dis-ease, the ways in which I had shaped my desires and disappointments into the depression that frames my way of being. What, I wanted to know, were the terms of my existence.

Although I had stopped being a diarist twenty years earlier, I had felt driven ever after—in fits and starts—to keep a journal of some sort, so I have a sketch, however spotty and faded, mapping my interior landscape. It has taken me a long time to learn to reread the signs. About five years ago I reread the early diaries and noted, "The me-ness of the diaries that disturbs me most is their now-ness—that is, the familiarity that I feel which arises not from memory but from currency. That Nancy all too often sounds like this Nancy, and I find myself thinking, Jesus, haven't I made any progress at all? I'm still falling in love, still thinking of death (tho' I don't wish for it so much any more, perhaps because I'm so much closer to it)." And just a few months ago, after reading them again: "That young woman strikes me thru' with horror and pity—her raw nerves, her clear-cut tho' undiagnosed depression, her sexual fears and frenzy. And I know that if I turned to my journal of 3 years ago, tho' the prose would be plainer I would still hear her shrieks and wails. . . . The diaries shriek fear. And a sense of failure. Things that are with me yet."

Things that will be, I see now, scrutinizing these texts that span more than a quarter of a century, with me forever. The terms of my existence: sickness, isolation, timidity, desire for death. They lie black as bars across the amazingly sunny landscape of a privileged life: good family, good education, good marriage, good jobs, good children. Since I don't believe in a depressive gene or genie, I must have chosen these terms myself. But who would make such a choice? Only a madwoman. But I'm not mad. You can take that as axiomatic. I've spent many years arriving at it, and it works. However comfortable an explanation madness might be, I can't have it.

Now that I've let go of madness, I can think about depression with more curiosity and less fear. It happens to an enormous number of us— millions and millions at any given moment. Most of us it happens to are women. Anything that strikes on such a massive scale cannot be purely idiosyncratic. Despite the personal features on some of my symptoms, my incarceration in Met State, emblematic of this wider prison of my life, was less a personal than a cultural event. I got there/here not because I am the one and only Nancy Mairs but because, in being Nancy Mairs, I reify—however idiosyncratically—the privileges, permissions, and denials that mold my type.

I am a kind of paralytic, my paralysis very characteristic of the depressed state. I don't dare move. "I am always afraid of losing things," I write in my journal. "What if I forget the names of the men I've slept with?" What if indeed. I don't know. But I catalogue these men and, at other points, all my past addresses, the cats who have lived with me, the poems I've published, my current blessings. Lists and lists, lest I forget. In one of Anaïs Nin's early diaries I come upon and jot down a quotation from E. Graham Howe: "The expression which is known as depression can be more clearly understood as coming to those who are not willing to be depressed, i.e.: to fall down according to the falling rhythm, or to let go when the time has come to lose. Depression is characteristically associated with over-conscientiousness, and so it is particularly liable to befall virtuous people. This is because they feel it is their moral duty to hang on to all good things, fixing them forever against the moving law of time."

Here I am: fixed in a graceful pose, my head thrown back, at the top of the field behind the house I was raised in, looking down the long slope across the greening, boggy bottom to the woods bronzed with last year's oak leaves still clinging, reddened with the new tips of maples, bearing bunches of my past like branches of lilacs, reeling at the fragrance, my arms pricked by the grey twigs, aching under the wet weight. But who am I, who am I, frozen in this pale light?

"I've never considered myself ordinary, average—," I write in my journal, "have always considered myself special in some way, destined for something—never sure what. But it would make a difference to the world somehow. Now I'm 33 years old, and it occurs to me that I probably won't ever do anything distinguished or lasting. I try to think of my raising my own children and educating others' in those terms, but it won't do—that's not what I had in mind; the gestures are too small." I'm on my trail at last, though not for several more years will I recognize myself: The Gifted Girl with Lots of Potential. Sure enough, still here. Only, as everyone knows, you can't at thirty-seven get away with what you got away with at seventeen. And after twenty years, the poor child is considerably the worse for wear.

She'd been an authentic creature once, though. What had happened to keep her hanging around so long after her time, frazzled, frayed, though with still an occasional quick grin of her girlish charm? From Patricia Meyer Spack's *The Female Imagination* I copy an insight into my journal: "Preservation of the feeling that one is set apart by special gifts depends often on failure to test those gifts, but the reluctance to test oneself generates guilt and disappointment. Unchallenged capacities fade away; it's harder and harder to believe in them. The world allows women not to use themselves, then denies their value because they fail to function fully." By the time I find it, I am too far gone into depression for any new understanding to brake my slide; but after I survive, and begin to emerge, it is still there, dated 4 September 1980, reminding me sternly that my time is up.

No more Gifted Girl with Lots of Potential. No more grandiose intentions of being a writer when I grow up, never realized because the products never come right and so I'm safer to sit still than to start the inevitable failure. This is all the grown up I get to be. No more "dream" world, more perfect than the "real" world, waiting if only I can find the small golden key: in which I love and rear my children without pain; in which I gratify my husband's slenderest desire; in which I dust all the surfaces in my room every morning instead of at Christmas and Easter; in which I understand how to solve a basic quadratic equation; in which someone discovers all the poems I haven't written and publishes them one after another in *The New Yorker*. There is one world—this world—and I have made it. No hope of a cure, ever, for being me.

In many ways these recognitions have been freeing. In my mushy adolescent meditation on "the border between this & that," for instance, I wrote that "more than carrying that into this, to gape at but never touch, I want that to be this, so that my dreams are tangible, so that I must not live always in my mind, existing only in my body. I want to unite my mind with my body, to be whole." Now that I know that the border I perceived was, like any border, an arbitrary political line inked across the geography of existence, I spend my mornings writing essays, then turn without disruption to the other tasks of inscribing a life. None of the writing is easy, but I no longer refuse to do it for fear that I'll fail to get it right. It can never be right, I know; it can only be done. Life as scribble. And the reverse.

But nothing I know can free me from depression, which is, by now at least, my existential style. It has infected me at the level of my nerve endings, and I will likely need, I am told, three tiny yellow pills with a glass of water at bedtime ever after if I am to survive. All the bars are in place, and the cement of guilt and disappointment is harder than any of the tools that I've found in here with me have been able to chip.

Still, of late I've felt a difference. I've begun to notice how large the space that encloses me seems to be. It's not a bad place really. The floors are polished, and the windows let in wide bands of light. I've put up no curtains but I've hung some tapestries on the walls into which are woven many fair women and many rhododendrons but no unicorns. I am mostly alone here, but occasional visitors float in and out bringing me chocolate ice cream sodas and fresh jokes. In the precise center of the room is a desk holding a black fountain pen, a bottle of black ink, and a stack of yellow legal-size pads, some of which are inscribed in a round black hand.

This place is real. I can live here. Come by, and I'll make you a cup of almond tea.

About the Author

NANCY MAIRS was born in Long Beach, California, in 1943, and grew up in New Hampshire and Massachusetts. She received the A.B. in English literature from Wheaton College (Massachusetts) in 1964. From 1966 to 1972 she worked as a technical editor at the Smithsonian Astrophysical Observatory, the MIT Press, and the Harvard Law School. In 1972 she moved to Tucson, Arizona, and taught high school and college composition courses while studying for the M.F.A. in creative writing (poetry) and the Ph.D. in English literature, which she was awarded in 1984. In the same year, her book of poems *In All the Rooms of the Yellow House* received first prize for poetry in the Western States Book Awards competition.